Overcoming Your Childhood Trauma

Overcoming Your Childhood Trauma

Trauma-Informed **Therapy Techniques and Exercises** to Support Deep Healing

Sostenes B. Lima, LCSW, and **Erica Lima, LCSW**

ZEITGEIST · NEW YORK

All rights reserved.
Published in the United States by Zeitgeist™, an imprint
and division of Penguin Random House LLC, New York.
zeitgeistpublishing.com

Zeitgeist™ is a trademark of Penguin Random House LLC.
The "Somatic Feel Wheel" chart by Erica Lima on pg. 60
is copyright © Erica Lima and appears here by permission.
ISBN: 9780593689936
Ebook ISBN: 9780593886359

Cover art © Shutterstock/Natalya Nepran
Interior art © Shutterstock/M.KOS, Shutterstock/Madua, Shutterstock/Natalya Nepran
Book design by Erin Yeung
Author photograph © by Tracy Battaglia at Fully Alive Photography
Edited by Clara Song Lee

Printed in the United States of America
1st Printing

For those who have journeyed
through deep despair and tragedy—
your refusal to give up is a testament
to your indomitable spirit.

CONTENTS

INTRODUCTION

The word "trauma" is derived from the Greek words τραύμα and titrōskein, which translate to "wound" and "to be wounded." These words call to mind two things: first, a sense of painful injury, often from serious physical or psychological harm, and second, the body and mind's amazing capacity to mend and heal, repairing whatever was damaged and restoring integrity and strength.

In our work as licensed therapists, we have seen firsthand how psychological trauma, which is a person's mental and emotional response to traumatic events in their past, can be healed and overcome when they receive proper care and support. Before opening our private practice, we spent many years working in different mental healthcare settings serving all kinds of populations, from immigrants and refugees to military veterans, people from the 2SLGBTQIA+ community, burned-out professionals, and folks struggling with substance abuse, severe mental illness, PTSD, and more. We soon recognized that despite the wide, complex range of their life experiences, our clients often shared certain similar responses to their pain—deep emotional trauma that left them questioning their experience, intuition, and capabilities, often at the expense of their health and relationships. For many, their trauma originated early in their life: childhood.

Childhood trauma occurs when a child witnesses or experiences an event (or multiple, ongoing events) that feels overwhelmingly painful and distressing, and is unable to process the event in a healthy way, causing parts of their development to become stuck. Children need safe environments and loving, attuned caregivers to help them make sense of their life experiences and recover from emotional distress and physical harm; without that proper care, they turn inward to adapt, creating coping mechanisms to protect themselves and disconnect from their pain. But just as physical wounds become vulnerable to infection if left unhealed over time, emotional wounds can create lasting problems, too. The early coping strategies that helped us survive as children can get in the way of our emotional, physical, and psychological development, and as adults, we may struggle to regulate our emotions, control unwanted behaviors, or manage physical issues like chronic pain and illness.

Fortunately, even the oldest wounds can be healed, and maladaptive mechanisms created in childhood can be unlearned and replaced with updated, healthier strategies that allow us to process our past, make meaningful changes in the present, and embrace a future that feels freer and more hopeful. Importantly, new research is showing that trauma healing work does not necessarily require revisiting traumatic experiences in painful detail or engaging deeply with the story of what happened.

In addition, because trauma involves multiple aspects of the mind and body, people often benefit from using multiple approaches to heal it, ranging from talk therapy and mindfulness to art therapy, trauma-informed yoga, and bodywork. In fact, prior to the rise of psychotherapy, cultures all around the world found hundreds of brilliant ways to heal trauma, ranging from movement, breathwork, and meditation to spiritual practices and ceremonies with sacred plant medicines.

As integrative psychotherapists who know how complicated and unique each person's healing journey can be, we are trained in multiple therapy modalities proven to support trauma healing, including attachment-based therapy, the Internal Family Systems Model (IFS), somatic (body-based) therapy, eye movement desensitization and reprocessing (EMDR), psychodynamic therapy, and mindfulness. (You'll learn more about each of these approaches later in the book.) We've leveraged our experience and knowledge to collect trauma-informed tools and exercises that meet you where you are, regardless of your background and life experiences.

While this book is not meant to be a replacement for professional therapy, its tools and exercises can help you make significant progress in processing your past and reducing symptoms and unwanted behaviors connected to it. If you choose to work with a licensed therapist to help you process whatever comes up, the results may be even more transformative.

How to Use This Book

This book is divided into four parts that guide you through important stages of the trauma healing journey. The parts are designed to be completed in order, so wait until you've completed parts one and two before moving on to the remaining parts.

Part One provides an overview of what lies ahead so that you can set reasonable expectations for yourself. They will help you gain a deeper understanding of childhood trauma, how to use a body-centered approach to healing, and how to mobilize your sense of self and become your own strongest ally.

Part Two helps you get in the habit of nurturing and supporting yourself. The exercises in this part are designed to be done in repetition, as often as you can. These exercises build the internal and external sense of grounding, safety, and security you need for trauma healing work. They also help you learn to pay attention to yourself so that you can be your own best guide. *If, at any point during the work, you feel too overwhelmed, dysregulated, or stuck to complete the exercises in part two, consider this a message from your psyche that you need more assistance than this book can provide, and seek the support of a trained mental health professional.*

Part Three takes you into the "wound healing" aspect of your work. Designed to bring attention to the parts of yourself that feel most damaged by the past, these exercises gently guide you into territory you may have tried to ignore or avoid. The work may feel uncomfortable at times, but this is also where significant relief can happen as you "discharge" or release heavy emotions and pain.

Part Four helps you strengthen your connection to your authentic self, who has always been within you—strong, whole, and unbroken—all this time. These exercises will help you feel empowered and whole again so that going forward you can tackle challenges more effectively and build healthier relationships with yourself and others.

While the exercises build upon one another and are therefore meant to be done in order, you can hold off on any that feel too triggering and move on to the next exercise. Then, when you feel ready, you can return to the one(s) you skipped.

When you are just beginning and are prompted by an exercise to recall an incident, it is best to work with memories that have a relatively low level of emotional intensity. You can determine this by rating your level of distress associated with the memory on a scale from 0 to 10, with 0 eliciting no emotional pain and 10 being the most emotionally painful. Start with memories you rate 2 or 3 on the distress scale and work your way up gradually as you feel ready.

If you begin feeling overwhelmed or distressed mid-exercise, there's no need to push through if that doesn't feel OK; take a moment to pause and ground yourself before continuing with the exercise (try the 5-4-3-2-1 Grounding Technique on page 66).

While working through the exercises, you need to be able to discern the difference between the normal discomfort that comes with healing and growth and the red-flag discomfort that comes from anything that is "too fast," "too much," or "too soon." The latter is a sign that you need to take a break, regroup, and seek more connection and support. (The Body Rhythm and Sensation Awareness exercise on page 57 will help you learn to identify different internal cues so that you can start making these distinctions.)

We invite you to tell the supportive people in your life that you've begun this work. This way, they can be there for you if you need assistance.

Healing trauma is a lifelong process, and it is not always linear. You will experience regressions and relapses and times when you want to completely avoid the work. This is normal and to be expected. Take your time as you move through this book. Ideally, spend two hours a week on the exercises, but if that doesn't feel doable, try to spend at least 30 minutes a week. By being consistent, you're letting yourself know that you are important enough to show up for.

Part One

Preparing to Heal

Chapter 1

Understanding Childhood Trauma

Traumatic experiences come in various shapes and sizes and can affect people differently. An experience that is traumatizing for one person might not be traumatizing for another (or might affect them to a lesser degree). This is because many factors come into play when we have an experience, including what has happened in our past, beliefs we hold, our present circumstances, the level at which we are able to tolerate distress, and how much support we have, just to name a few.

"Big-*T* trauma" refers to major life-threatening events and debilitating issues such as physical or sexual abuse, physical abandonment, natural disaster, war, experiencing or witnessing a violent crime, chronic physical neglect, and so on. Meanwhile, "little-*t* trauma" arises from events that society views as less life-threatening and/or dramatic. However, even little-*t* trauma can be psychologically distressing, particularly when these "little" traumas occur repeatedly over time or intensely in a short period. Little-*t* traumas can include emotional neglect, emotional abuse, parental divorce, bullying, financial woes, the death of a pet, and many more.

Regardless of how "big" or "little" a person's traumatic experiences are, the consequences of childhood trauma are generally the same: long-lasting effects that can wreak havoc on a person's mental, emotional, and physical health.

Permission to Release Survival Mode

Whether it's anxiety or depression, perfectionism or people-pleasing, self-sabotage, problems with executive functioning skills, or medical issues like chronic pain or autoimmune illnesses, childhood trauma can show up in adult life in myriad ways. However, if we view the body as an organism with an innate ability to adapt, we can see that these effects are all normal, understandable responses to trauma and stress. The body had to protect, dissociate (i.e., "disconnect" mind from body), and become hypervigilant to survive the stress it was experiencing. It had to respond protectively in the face of a distressing environment(s) and/or relationship(s).

Having childhood trauma is not a character weakness, personal flaw, or deficit—our bodies were designed to go into "survival mode" to protect us from repeated pain, stress, and suffering. But even as we honor our bodies for these superpowers, we also recognize how painful, frustrating, and exhausting it can be to feel and live this way. When worn for too long, protective armor can feel heavy and restrictive.

We invite you to give yourself permission to make time and space to learn new, more helpful ways to experience yourself and your past. Over time, you may be able to remove your armor and still feel safe and whole in your body. Everyone deserves this freedom—and you are no exception.

The Traumatized Mind-Body

Having positive, healthy relationships with adult caregivers during our formative years is profoundly important. Such relationships foster a positive sense of self and create closeness and connection in our relationships. They also increase our ability to be in the present moment, help us learn to manage difficult emotions (e.g., anger, sadness, and disappointment), and can even reduce the likelihood of health issues later. However, when there is significant impairment or neglect in our relationships with our adult caregivers and others, our ability to understand in a healthy way who we are in relation to the outside world is lost.

The research of revolutionary trauma experts such as Bessel van der Kolk, Judith Lewis Herman, Resmaa Menakem, Dr. Thema Bryant, Nadine Burke Harris, and others has shed light on how the effects of traumatic experiences are stored in the tissues of the brain and body, where they can affect the entire autonomic nervous system (ANS). The ANS is the system of nerves throughout the body that controls all our unconscious processes—from our heartbeat, lungs, and digestion to our immune system and reproductive functions.

According to these experts, repeated and prolonged exposure to traumatic events impacts the neuropathways in our brain, creating lasting imprints that have a cascading effect on the body. This is particularly true during childhood when the brain is still developing. Emotional trauma can alter the brain's structure, changing the way it functions.

Areas of the brain responsible for processing emotions like fear and anger can become overactive, leading the brain to be constantly on alert for threats, while other areas responsible for memory formation and retrieval may experience volume loss or function abnormally, as with intrusive thoughts or difficulty recalling memories. The brain area responsible for executive functioning skills like impulse control, emotional regulation, and decision-making may be underdeveloped. In addition, high levels of stress hormones can lead to hormone imbalances that negatively impact the immune system. There can also be imbalances in mood-influencing neurotransmitters like serotonin and dopamine, which can contribute to mental health conditions such as anxiety and depression.

Psychologically, the unconscious mind will block or dissociate from the body anytime it experiences traumatic events or something that subconsciously reminds it of these traumatic events. Over time, this alters our ability to understand our emotions and attach or bond with others to form healthy, meaningful relationships. As the brain rewires itself to stay in survival mode, feelings of detachment or dissociation arise, as do problems with learning, focusing, and/or controlling impulses.

In its effort to avoid the pain of the past, the mind creates a disconnection or separation from the younger part of ourselves who experienced it. All this can lead to an inability to form a healthy sense of self, which can result in low self-esteem and increased feelings of shame and guilt, and disconnect us from our humanity so that we can't experience the full spectrum of our emotions or the deep sense of feeling fully whole and "alive."

In addition, trauma has a multilayered, multigenerational impact that can affect multiple parts of our identity. It is not only an external experience caused by people, places, or the world, but also an internal experience that can be re-created again and again. Trauma that occurs during the developmental stages of childhood becomes locked in our minds and bodies with qualities that inevitably resemble the age we were when the wounding occurred.

For example, imagine a four-year-old boy who is excited to serve himself dinner for the first time. Gripping the ladle tightly, he slowly scoops the food into his bowl and feels elated when he succeeds, completing a new task he's watched numerous adults do effortlessly. With confidence soaring, he hurries toward the dining table to show his parents what he's achieved. Suddenly, he trips and drops his bowl, splattering food all over the kitchen floor. He hears a loud sigh of annoyance and a groan of frustration, and when he sees the disappointment in his parents' eyes, his body immediately tenses up, locking his arms and legs.

The four-year-old covers his face and runs to hide. The feeling of shame, the thoughts of "I am a disappointment; I can't do anything right; something must be wrong with me" begin to set in. The lingering impact of his parents' disapproval weighs heavily on him when his parents fail to repair their initial response of disapproval and disappointment. The seed of an idea—that there is something wrong or defective about him—has been planted, and it is watered every time similar responses to innocent mistakes are normalized in the household.

As the feeling of shame is imprinted into the four-year-old's nervous system, it creates a narrative that eventually becomes a bullying inner critic when he is older. Now the critic part has to protect him from ever feeling that sense of defectiveness again, so it lashes out harshly to make sure he never fails again. As a teenager, he becomes afraid of "getting in trouble" or upsetting anyone, often lying to hide anything potentially negative about himself. In adulthood, he works overtime frequently and tries to control as many aspects of his life as he can, even though this creates serious anxiety.

Now imagine this same person, who experienced repeated emotional neglect because of their parents' constant disapproval, has now been pushed into assuming the role of caretaker for one of their parents. They find themselves feeling self-mistrust and self-abandonment for agreeing to such a choice even though a big part of them didn't want to. Perhaps their inner critic berates them for having these feelings, too. The four-year-old has become an adult who struggles to get their needs met in relationships, has difficulty with decision-making, and often feels hollow and detached from themselves. Not only has their trauma impacted their body, but it has also caused them to internalize harmful beliefs that affect how they feel about themselves. This leads them to unconsciously repeat behaviors over and over, including a harsh and unforgiving approach to raising their own children. This is a common trauma response caused by the subconscious desire to process or work through pain so that it can be healed.

Trauma's impact influences us psychologically, physiologically, emotionally, and even spiritually. It can stunt the maturation and development process, leaving us stuck in patterns we cannot break out of (i.e., arrested development). This can show up as the inability to receive love or support, profound negative self-esteem, persistent procrastination, avoidance of intimate relationships, inability to trust or rely on others, and remaining small to prevent failure or rejection. These internal ruptures destroy our trust in ourselves and can cause us to feel insecure about who we are, how we show up in the world, and who we can trust. This disconnection is the body's way of keeping us safe, yet it has a lasting impact on our ability to trust and connect with others in a meaningful way as adults.

What Healing Looks Like

Acknowledging your history and your experience is the first step in addressing the negative impacts of trauma on your life. Just as you'd change the bandage of a physical wound and treat any infections, seeking help and doing the exercises in this book can be a helpful step in finding "wound care" for your trauma. In our practice and in this book, we use a holistic approach that acknowledges the impact of trauma on both the brain and body and helps you finally create some of the conditions you needed but did not have during childhood. This gives you the opportunity to build new, positive pathways in your brain and body so you can start feeling connection, safety, and stability in your life. Research has shown that even small moments of fostering these conditions can have a profoundly healing impact on the brain as well as on the autonomic nervous system. Engaging consistently and compassionately in this self-healing work can be deeply transformative.

It is normal to feel overwhelmed by the topic of healing trauma and the possibility of resolving decades' worth of conditioned thinking, reacting, and responding due to traumatic experiences. In our practice, when we meet with a client for the first time, we help them set expectations by discussing why healing is not a linear process, and with that in mind, we stress the benefits of being consistent with therapy appointments even when the client might feel a sense of dread about showing up. We also share that often, after a client has attended three to six months of therapy, they may get an urge to quit or even develop feelings of anger toward their therapist. Again, this is normal and to be expected. Surprisingly, these feelings actually signal a time for optimal healing—so long as the client keeps showing up and is honest about what's happening for them.

This book functions similarly. After some time or perhaps at the outset, you may develop negative feelings toward the book and exercises and/or feel an urge to discontinue the work. When that happens, it can be helpful to take some time to journal about your feelings, do something that helps release the feelings, or bring in curiosity about what might be causing this urge. If you can, keep showing up, even if you can't get past the grounding exercises until months later. Any engagement with these exercises (or with trauma therapy in general) counts as progress. Success is not measured by plowing through a book or claiming mastery over something. Rather, it is demonstrated by your commitment to yourself, your voice, your experience, your body, and your healing.

The challenging thing about healing trauma is that it cannot be rushed. So many of us wish we could feel relief *yesterday* without the scary work of facing our deepest fears and pain. However, with consistent practice, as you build up your internal and external resources (which we guide you to do in the upcoming chapters), the healing work does get easier, or at least more tolerable. As you express your pain and begin to feel seen and witnessed (even if it's only by yourself), a powerful sense of relief will well up and new clarity and insight will rise to the surface, encouraging you to keep doing the work.

Helpful Coping Statements

During the process of healing trauma, some things are within your control, and some are not. You can develop some control over your mindset, how you spend your energy and time, the boundaries you set, and other parts of your life where you have some agency and decision-making power. However, you cannot control other aspects of your experience, such as changing the past, predicting the future, and other people's thoughts, feelings, and behaviors about you. Accepting this lack of control can be tough. Use the following coping statements whenever you need a reminder of what you can and cannot control during this process.

Healing takes as long as it takes.

When we are dealing with the autonomic nervous system, we are dealing with a system that cannot be consciously controlled. Knowing this, we can begin to honor our own unique needs and pace and start the work of dismantling a key part of trauma—the trauma of being pressured, forced, or made to conform in a way that's out of alignment with our wants or needs. When it comes to your healing journey, resting, taking breaks, stopping during an exercise, and hitting the pause button so you can address other life events and demands are all essential parts of this work. There's no need to follow the pace set by others when digesting material or participating in healing experiences.

My body is doing the best it can—thus, I am doing the best I can.

In any given moment, your mind and body are doing the best they can with whatever resources are available. Just as you cannot control the pace of healing, you also cannot force your body to do more than it is already trying to do. It is doing everything it can to keep you alive, and for that, it deserves honor and respect. This is a reality worth remembering when you are feeling particularly challenged and hard on yourself.

I aim for progress over perfection.

Due to how complex and unique our individual identities are, there is no one-size-fits-all or perfect way to engage with any healing practices or materials. There is also no way of healing perfectly, and deep wounds typically take a long time to heal. Change will not happen overnight, and the progress you may notice is likely to occur in small ways, or glimmers, initially.

I practice self-compassion, which is crucial to my healing work.

Working through childhood experiences will often feel draining, defeating, and discouraging. It is completely normal for such feelings to arise—especially in anyone who has relied heavily on strategies to avoid or deny their trauma-related challenges. When this is the case, it's essential to practice self-compassion. Give yourself grace. You can do this by showing empathy to the parts of you that feel drained, defeated, or discouraged. You can tell yourself that it's OK to feel whatever you are feeling, and that it is also OK not to know exactly what is happening to you. Show yourself this same self-compassion as you approach the exercises in part two. Carve out time and space to connect with and nurture yourself as you move forward. With repeated practice, you will develop invaluable lifelong skills.

Chapter 2
Your Unique Healing Journey

To practice showing up for yourself, it's important to establish a rhythm with which you will engage with this book. Prioritize your mental health by being flexible around your schedule and expectations, carving out time and space to do the exercises, and devoting sufficient energy to this process of connecting to yourself.

Here are five tips to help you jump-start your practice and get the rhythm going:

1. **Location:** Pick a convenient location that feels safe, supportive, calm, nurturing, and private. This could be a bedroom corner, a patio chair, or sometimes even a park bench. The space should be free of distractions and offer you the option to sit, lie down, move around, or journal as called for by the various exercises.

Identify one or more of these spaces so that if one is unavailable or you need more space for a particular exercise, you have a choice.

2. **Time:** Block off time on your calendar, ideally for at least two hours each week, to have a "date" with yourself. This can be done in increments—perhaps 20 minutes one day, 45 minutes another day, etc. Each exercise has a suggested duration, which includes at least 10 minutes for journaling. Feel free to extend your journaling time for as long as you'd like or have time for. Use reminders on your phone to alert you when the time you set aside for yourself is drawing near. Then spend that time doing one of the exercises in this book.

3. **Accountability:** Tell a close friend that you are beginning this work. Ask them to check in with you occasionally to see how you are doing. Ask them if you can turn to them for support and encouragement when the work and feelings that arise feel tough or discouraging and give them an idea of what support and encouragement might look and sound like for you.

4. **Reminder:** Record a video or write a letter to your future self about the meaning that doing this work has for you. Share your motivation and goals for engaging with this book. Set an intention for what progress might look like. Watch the video or read the letter when you feel stuck or uncertain.

5. **Motivation:** Think beyond today. Visualize the next three generations who will benefit from your time and energy to break cycles and heal yourself and/or acknowledge your contribution to the social healing legacy, which your community, your culture, and the world will benefit from.

Feeling Safe and Getting Help

The exercises in this book have been chosen to support you in resolving aspects of your childhood trauma. If you start feeling overwhelmed, detached from your environment/body, or experience panic, do the 5-4-3-2-1 Grounding Technique on page 66, phone a friend, or reach out to a therapist for help. While the exercises are designed for safety and comfort, if you experience a life-threatening emergency, call 911 or go to your nearest emergency room.

Humans are hardwired for social support, so there are no benefits to managing difficult challenges without help. We hope you will seek out the support you need. Here are a few mental health resources to reach out to, if needed:

- **988 Suicide & Crisis Lifeline:** Dial or text 988 if you have thoughts of suicide or are experiencing a mental health crisis; available 24/7.

- **NAMI HelpLine:** Call 1-800-950-NAMI (6264), text "HelpLine" to 62640, or email helpline@nami.org for emotional support.

- **Crisis Text Line:** Text HOME to 741-741 to connect with a trained crisis counselor via text message, 24/7.

- **National Domestic Violence Hotline:** Call 800-799-SAFE (7233). Advocates are available 24/7 to provide confidential support to anyone experiencing domestic violence or seeking resources and information.

- **National Sexual Assault Hotline:** Call 800-656-HOPE (4673) to connect with a trained staff member from a sexual assault service provider in your area 24/7. Crisis chat support is available at hotline.rainn.org.

- **The Trevor Project:** Call 866-488-7386 or text START to 678-678. Crisis counselors support young LGBTQ people who are in crisis by being accessible 24/7. Crisis chat support is available at TheTrevor-Project.org/get-help.

Taking a Mind-Body Approach

During periods of extreme stress, the brain's ability to regulate itself in response to perceived threats becomes compromised; it can even go offline completely. This is because when the body's alarm system is activated, the fight, flight, or freeze response is triggered and our primitive instincts are activated—we must either fight, run away, or "play dead." Our cognitive ability to reason, make decisions, and control impulses is temporarily blocked, allowing the body to default to its instinctual reactions to ensure our safety.

While this is a protective mechanism that is meant to prevent harm or additional trauma, it can become a conditioned reaction that does not serve us in our adult life. In this book, we integrate a somatic, or body-based, approach with a cognitive one, weaving together these two aspects by helping you increase your somatic awareness of your body's sensations while you form a new relationship with yourself and your perception of the past. By developing cognition (active thinking) around your body's experience and reactions, you will have more of a say-so, or voice, around your story and how you respond to stress in the future.

The upcoming exercises allow for reflection and understanding around traumatic experiences while providing a secure sense of access to your body to prevent retraumatization. You will develop the ability to talk about difficult situations from your past. However, because your body has likely been conditioned to react in a certain way, avoid pushing too hard to connect or speed up when you are processing your experiences.

How Is This Approach Different?

Many trauma treatments have historically avoided or intellectualized a client's physiological or body-based experiences rather than incorporating both experiences into the treatment modality. Such treatments include:

- Cognitive-centered treatments, such as cognitive behavioral therapy (CBT), which focuses on reframing and replacing negative thought patterns that lead to unwanted behaviors.

- Psychoanalysis, where the client explores the mind and their relationships with their parents/caregivers and the unconscious to gain insight into behavior and emotions.

- Behaviorism-based therapies, such as prolonged exposure therapies, where the focus is on gradually exposing the client to their triggers to assist them in overcoming the triggers and learn new strategies and emotional regulation.

Even though these theories acknowledge that we store trauma in our bodies and they can be immensely helpful, they bypass listening and working with the body by focusing more on verbalizing the experiences or learning emotional regulation skills. They all share a similar emphasis on the role of the brain's cognitive processing, as if it were possible to reason and think one's way out of trauma.

Today's trauma experts believe that these approaches sometimes have limited success. One such expert, psychiatrist Bessel van der Kolk, emphasized the value of paying attention to the body—how it stores information and holds traumatic memory—in the treatment of trauma. Because stressful, traumatic situations have a profound impact on the body, engaging the body can help release and heal trauma that may be blocked from consciousness by opening pathways that allow stuck energy to flow.

Healing the Cognitive Mind

Throughout childhood, we develop beliefs about ourselves and the world around us based on our experiences and relationships. Often referred to as core beliefs, they develop during our formative years and are usually absolute, binary beliefs. While some therapies label certain core beliefs as inherently bad or wrong and then focus on trying to eradicate them, we invite you to consider an alternative perspective:

Your core beliefs reflected your experiences and relationships at a time when you were trying to make sense of your painful experiences but were still too young to have the appropriate connection and context to process negative experiences. As a result, you blamed yourself (as children do) and altered your behavior to try to ensure that you would not be abandoned by your caregiver(s). At the time, this altered behavior, which formed one of your core beliefs, was protective and reflexive rather than defective.

For example, if a parent is emotionally neglectful and repeatedly downplays their child's experience whenever the child is upset, and says something like "You're making a big deal about nothing," the child may develop a core belief such as "There is something wrong with me." When a parent repeatedly withholds validation of their child's painful experience, the child comes to believe that they are unworthy of support and validation and will now make decisions and engage in behaviors that no longer require those things from their parents. This is an adaptive response to the persistent neglect, but the wound of feeling "There is something wrong with me" gets embedded into the child's belief system.

Each core belief has a backstory that often goes unnoticed or is never understood. These unprocessed beliefs get frozen in time, coloring how we relate to others and every experience we have moving forward. While working through this book, you will learn to unpack, discover, discharge, and replace outdated core beliefs, or belief systems, that no longer serve you.

These types of wounds take time to feel, heal, and release. Certain types of talk therapy like the Internal Family Systems Model (IFS) of psychotherapy and psychodynamic therapy allow for the dark corners of these wounds to be witnessed, heard, and safely contained. For example, in Internal Family Systems therapy, you start noticing and getting to know shadow parts, or exiled parts, of yourself—e.g., the part of you that may believe "There is something wrong with me," as in the previous example. You start to understand why these parts are there and why they show up. Similarly, in psychodynamic therapy, you may become aware of childhood wounds and learn to sit with them while processing the memories in a safe environment; you can also learn to recognize your defense mechanisms, or ways that your mind defends or protects itself from these dark corners, when triggers show up for you. This creates new experiences that replace the painful experiences of your childhood with connection and support in the present.

This connection and support can come from working with a trusted therapist, but it can also come from working with yourself on your own as you gradually become aware of, understand, and feel compassion for the "bad," or shadow, parts of yourself. When you carefully and safely visit old wounds, there's an expansion in your sense of awareness and emotional stability. The wounded parts no longer go unnoticed and you're able to witness them and build compassion for your younger self. This is one of the reasons why people usually experience relief after sharing a painful experience, either with another person or alone, as with journaling.

Processing Trauma in the Body

If you have ever said to yourself, "I wish this didn't bother me so much" or "I can't seem to move past this experience," you may have wanted to *think* your way out of an emotional or visceral experience. The logical brain has a way of digesting information and then "moving on" from the experience far more quickly than the body can. This is because the body speaks a very different language, which many people are not yet attuned to. Anything the body perceives as too fast, too soon, or too much can cause the autonomic nervous system to initiate the fight, flight, or freeze response, which may later manifest as lingering aches, pain, stiffness, or dissociation.

One of the goals of trauma work is to develop attunement between mind and body. This increases awareness and connectivity between mind and body, helping to heal any tension and trauma the body is holding. A leading innovator in couples therapy, Sue Johnson, uses the metaphor of learning the tango as an example of how attunement between couples can help them work out their inner traumas. We feel this metaphor is applicable to the relationship between body and mind, as well. While it's likely the duo will step on each other's toes from time to time or one may want to rush off the dance floor on occasion, the commitment to learning to dance together provides the mind and body an important opportunity to work out trauma and move past it. Learning to dance as partners involves several basic steps: tuning in to, or hearing, the music (i.e., noticing your feelings and experiences); feeling the rhythm (i.e., validating your feelings and experiences); moving your body (i.e., encountering and self-soothing); and acknowledging and responding to your partner's movements and vice versa (i.e., integrating body and mind into your overall self).

There are numerous ways to connect to one's body that have been developed and used over the centuries, but in this book, we are specifically exploring certain therapeutic options, including somatic-based therapies, bilateral stimulation, mindfulness, attachment-based therapy, and the Internal Family Systems Model (IFS). We do, however, want to acknowledge and pay respect to the many indigenous, Afrocentric, Asiatic, and other historically marginalized groups who have used trauma healing practices for millennia, often integrating the body and mind in their healing practices in brilliant ways.

Growing Emotional Intelligence

The repercussions of childhood trauma are strong adaptive responses: the child shields themselves from emotional pain or creates an internal need of reassurance from others. For example, a child who repeatedly experiences rejection and invalidation learns to pull away, trust only themselves, and builds an emotional barrier around themselves in an effort to keep others from inflicting more pain. Or a child whose caregiver is unpredictable, with moments of affection followed by droughts of disconnection, develops an adaptive response of seeking approval and validation from others as a form of security; perhaps they try to anticipate cues or read facial expressions for signs of looming emotional abandonment and then engage in different behaviors to try to stop this abandonment from happening.

These relational childhood traumas can hinder the development of emotional connections and secure bonds, which are essential for healthy development. This is why you may feel like a five-year-old in an adult body who wants to run and hide if someone scolds you. Relearning the skills and missed experiences within a therapeutic space is crucial for healing childhood trauma. The exercises in this book help you re-create meaningful experiences with yourself to replace negative experiences of shame, neglect, or other abuse. Additionally, using these tools consistently and repeatedly will allow the new skills to be strengthened, replacing old, wounded reactions with more emotionally mature responses and an emotionally healed internal space.

While therapies such as narrative therapy, psychodynamic therapy, and Internal Family Systems are useful for addressing missed experiences in childhood as well as processing experiences of toxic shame and stunted emotional growth, attachment-based therapy is a key modality here. It is a relational approach that contextualizes a person's first relationships (usually between the caregiver and the child) and seeks to explore, process, and repair those early emotional relationship wounds. Placing high importance on a person's initial experience with people and the world around them, attachment-based therapy seeks to re-create a safe, supportive, bonded relationship that is alive and growing in the present.

Rewiring Habitual Mind-Body Reactions

You may be aware of some of your reflexive responses to a perceived risk or danger. Perhaps you reflexively apologize to or console others, fearful of being cut off or abandoned. Or perhaps you reflexively pull away from conflict or overwhelm in your environment. It's also possible that you don't recognize your reflexive responses right now, and that's OK. You'll have an opportunity to start becoming aware of them later.

Babies and toddlers learn to cope and self-soothe from their caregivers. If they are not soothed by their caregivers and these skills are not taught, they can grow into middle-school-aged kids with big emotions without the skills to regulate themselves. The middle schooler may then be perceived as "acting out," "being disruptive," or "seeking attention" and is further alienated from the connection and support they actually need. The child learns that adults are not there for them, and they become hyperaware of any potential threat or negative stimuli, resulting in suppression of their true feelings or in disconnection from themselves altogether.

When they reach adulthood, this child may have a deeply ingrained belief that adults are not available, cannot be trusted, and are not interested in meeting their needs. They may also have had numerous experiences to further validate this belief and make it harder to release. However, if they learn the skills of responding to themselves, validating their own needs, and acknowledging and allowing themselves to have needs, they can become more open to the idea that underneath their hard exterior is a distraught, lonely, and scared toddler with big emotions who is waiting to be scooped up and held.

A modality that is particularly helpful with entrenched beliefs from childhood stemming from traumatic experiences is the Internal Family Systems Model (IFS), developed by Richard C. Schwartz in the 1980s.

This model of psychotherapy brings to light the origins of wounds, what protects these wounds, and what prevents them from being re-wounded, ultimately helping the client address the needs of their wounded inner child. You'll encounter a few IFS-based exercises in later chapters that will guide you in the process of nurturing and re-parenting your wounded inner child.

Rebuilding Healthy Connections

One reason it is difficult for folks with a history of childhood trauma to form and maintain meaningful connections with others is that our most important experiences are developed through our connection, or lack thereof, to our primary caregivers. These are the blueprints of our relationships, and we learn from these relationships what parts of ourselves are accepted, what parts are unwelcome, and how we must adapt to survive. Can we lean on others in times of distress, or must we find independence within ourselves? Perhaps we learn to not have any needs at all to avoid burdening others.

Trauma healing work begins to reorganize and reconstruct these blueprints of relationships, creating a gradual change, harmony, and acceptance within us. For example, some people are highly sensitive and may need more space, permission, and attunement than others to heal. There is no "one way" to heal the trauma. In fact, part of the healing process in therapy involves working with each person's subjective experience and figuring out their unique needs and what tools and techniques work best for them. Attachment-based therapy directly supports healing trauma work in this way, as it allows the therapist to cater the relationship to the client's needs and experiences, thereby fostering a restorative experience.

Uncovering Your Authentic Self

Engaging in this work and committing to heal your childhood trauma not only breaks cycles of trauma for the next generation but also has a positive impact that will serve you through the rest of your life. Although it may take time to notice the changes, your relationship to yourself and others will reap lifelong benefits.

The fact that a part of you believes in your capacity to heal traumatic wounds and has picked up this book is indicative of the power of healing within you. Consider a stormy and cloudy day, or perhaps a storm that has been ongoing for some time. You may see glimmers of the sun, but due to all the clouds, it is hard to see the light of the sun shining fully. The sun resembles our authentic self, which is always present, even in times of storm, fog, or blizzards. This self is innately wise, strong, undamaged, and whole, and it is always within us, although it may have been obscured for a long time.

Our desire is for you to see your true, actualized self and to become aware of your innate drive to be your best self. Your efforts toward personal growth and discovery shed light on your inherently good self. Throughout this book and your journey to heal childhood trauma, you will notice glimmers of relief, a shift in perspective, more spaciousness, an increased sense of harmony, increased empathy, and more acceptance toward yourself and others.

Unexpected Superpowers

These new connections to your authentic self will lead to "unexpected superpowers," because they will create an internal anchor that grounds you and becomes a source of support that is always with you, available to provide healing energy anytime you need it. This will help keep you from being swayed by unfit influences and will decrease guilt, leading to more self-confidence and self-assurance. The glimmers of hope we mentioned are new and different connections to yourself. Here are some of the ways they may show up:

- Decreased reactivity; an increased ability to pause and choose

- Increased internal power; a sense of control over your thoughts, feelings, and actions (i.e., a sense of agency)

- Increased connection and intimacy with people in your life

- Deeper experience of joy, gratitude, and acceptance

- Sense of internal harmony

- Ease and permission just to be

- Finding your voice, your personality, and your opinions

- Compassionate understanding of your emotional experience

- Increased sense of self-compassion

- Increased spaciousness and capacity to hold difficult feelings and conversations

Common Questions or Concerns

Will I still be able to do this work if I am short on time?

While this book was designed for people who may not have access to therapy services, you can expect this book to require as much time as a recurring therapy appointment. The emotions evoked by this book's exercises will require your attention and time to support, ground, and reorient yourself. If you cannot devote the suggested two hours each week, we suggest dedicating at least 30 minutes a week to this book and to yourself. It's important to be consistent throughout this process, as doing so reminds your mind and body that you are important enough to show up for.

Can I still do these exercises if I am already in therapy?

Absolutely! This book works best when you have a therapist so that you can further process the content and whatever comes up for you. Although it is not required to have a therapist to practice these exercises, we do recommend access to one if possible.

If I am unable to do mindfulness or bodywork, should I still do the exercises?

If you cannot do mindfulness or any type of bodywork (i.e., somatic therapy exercises), we will offer modifications that allow you to engage mindfully in an external way instead of internally. Use the modifications within the book, and do not force yourself to engage in mindfulness or somatic-based exercises if this is very triggering for you.

Can I skip around or do I need to follow the order of the book?

This book is designed with specific exercises that build upon each other. The exercises at the beginning of the book are meant to serve as a foundation for later exercises. However, if you already have experience with grounding and mindfulness activities, you can move on to part three.

Should I create goals or expectations for myself while I use this book?

Some folks are more goal-oriented whereas others do not see healing linearly. If you want to set goals for yourself, use the SMART goal-setting concept: SMART goals are Specific, Measurable, Achievable, Relevant, and Time-bound.

How often should I do the exercises? Can I do some more than once?

Most of these exercises are intended to help you cultivate a way of life through repeated practice, rather than through something you do just once. For example, you can engage with the grounding or mindfulness exercises two to three times a week. The goal is to create a practice where you mindfully and continuously tend to yourself. That said, some of the more in-depth exercises may only need to be done once; however, you may find approaching them a second time in a therapeutic setting may help you process their content in more depth.

What if some exercises are triggering?

The first five exercises are grounding and stabilizing exercises meant to help you regulate in moments of distress. Remember, be gentle with yourself; do not attempt to rush through this. Complete what you can without feeling the need to push through. If these initial exercises are too triggering to even attempt, consider enlisting the help of a licensed mental health professional to support you. If a later exercise is triggering but the initial exercises were not, you can go back to one of the initial exercises to see if it helps you regulate before returning to the later exercise. If not, you can revisit the triggering exercise another time.

Signs of Progress in Recovery

Although progress looks different depending on the person, there are some signs of progress that you will be able to take note of.

Signs of Progress in Early Recovery

- You feel more confident identifying and naming your feelings.

- You have more self-compassion and understanding toward yourself and your experiences.

- You have less self-doubt and more self-confidence.

- You feel more in touch with your needs and wants.

- You have a heightened sense of curiosity toward yourself and others.

- You feel more at ease when creating boundaries for yourself.

- You can identify and react less to your triggers.

Signs of Progress in Late Recovery

- You feel you can advocate on behalf of your own needs and wants.

- You worry less about what others think and are more connected to your own experience.

- You blame yourself less and have more sympathy for mistakes and errors you make.

- You have more internal space for other people's triggers and emotions.

- You can see others through a lens of trauma, increasing a sense of empathy toward others.

- You can dream and take up more space and time for yourself.

- You can find your way back to regulation, calm, and internal harmony when you feel dysregulated.

Part Two

Building Up Your Resources

Chapter 3

Developing Your Internal Tools

Internal resources are tools that provide, among other qualities, feelings of support and safety. These resources lay the foundation for trauma therapy and other types of healing work. Childhood trauma essentially disconnects or cuts us off from accessing these internal resources, but they can always be learned and practiced. Internal resources include connecting to your body and your sense of self from a full and embodied place. Some examples include mindfulness, meditation, somatic touch, spiritual practices, and breathwork.

When used, these resources reinforce a sense of safety, connection, control and agency, empowerment, aliveness, and self-awareness. This increases your ability to move through difficult emotions and memories while still maintaining a sense of security, stability, and connectedness to your adult self in the present moment. What's more, relying on internal resources such as mindfulness can improve focus and concentration, reduce impulsivity and reactivity, increase feelings of connectedness, decrease symptoms of anxiety and depression, and even improve immune system function.

Acceptance Breath

What You'll Need

- 20 to 30 minutes of uninterrupted time
- Pillow or blanket (optional)
- Journal and pen/pencil (or digital)

THIS EXERCISE INCREASES your awareness of your breath and how accepting the experience can bring about physical changes in your body and your conscious state. The goal is not to change or alter the breath, but to practice noticing the breath as is.

Explore the breath and its impact with curiosity. Be patient with yourself as you adjust to this new way of engaging with yourself, simply noticing your tendencies around your breath and any small changes that might naturally occur. You are developing the skill of meeting yourself and your body exactly where you are. This will naturally soften and relax the tension in your body without a directive to "change something."

Breathwork (*pranayama*) has its roots in Hindu, Taoist, and Buddhist traditions, where it helps the practitioner reclaim connection and control over their breath not only for better physical health but also for spiritual growth. The practice of connecting to and bringing our awareness to the breath serves as an internal regulator, where the breath becomes a stabilizing force and presence. Interestingly, the rhythm of the breath's expansion and contraction resembles other patterns in nature—the tide, the turn of the seasons, and the change from day to night.

Note Give yourself plenty of time and space when you are first learning breathwork. Later, you can engage with your breath anywhere. Acceptance Breath is an excellent tool to use after any of the other exercises in this book, especially if you feel dysregulated or overwhelmed. If you become anxious while doing this exercise, move or shake your body to orient yourself to your physical surroundings.

Instructions

1. Sit or lie in a comfortable position in your favorite calm, quiet space. Use a pillow or blanket for comfort, if desired, and close your eyes or gaze down if that's more comfortable for you.

2. Place your hand on your stomach or chest to bring your awareness into your body. There is no need to change or alter your breath.

3. As you breathe in, say hello to the breath. Track where the breath enters and travels through your body—from your nose to the back of your throat, to your chest, and so on.

4. As you exhale, follow the path the breath takes until it exits your body.

5. Acknowledge, notice, and track the expansion and contraction of the breath. Does it have a temperature? Any other qualities? Notice how your body responds to the breath.

6. Continue acknowledging and following your breath in and out for the duration of the time you set aside.

7. When you are ready, bring your awareness to your fingers and toes and slowly connect to your surroundings. Orient yourself by noticing objects, colors, and textures in your environment.

Journal Prompt

Describe your experience of connecting to your breath. What urges or impulses, if any, did you experience as you were engaging with your breath? What did you like or not like about this experience? What changes, if any, did you notice in your body as you focused on your breath?

Safe Place

What You'll Need

- 20 to 30 minutes of uninterrupted time
- Objects that signal safety and comfort (e.g., blanket, pillow, plant, stuffed animal)
- Journal and pen/pencil (or digital)

BECOMING ANCHORED IN the mind-body connection, guided imagery, or visualization can have profound positive physiological effects on the body. This is because the mind and body can make sensory experiences real regardless of how they originate—for example, visualize your favorite food; your mouth will likely water and you can even "taste" the flavors. When we position ourselves to access and experience safety in our minds, we experience safety in our bodies. Because guided imagery engages the autonomic nervous system, it can alter our emotional states—feeling calm physiologically has a powerful impact on emotional wellness.

This exercise guides you through the process of visualizing a safe place in your mind that you can access whenever you need to. It can be used during times of distress, discomfort, overwhelm, stress, emotional dysregulation, anxiety, and panic to calm the body's fight, flight, or freeze response. This inner resource can be incredibly helpful when engaging in trauma healing work, and we suggest you use it to complement the other exercises in this book. The more you use this safe place, the greater the sense of safety it offers.

Note If it is too triggering or overwhelming to do mindfulness exercises or guided meditations with your eyes closed, keep your eyes open and your gaze low, try one of the modifications, or get support from a mental health professional around using these types of tools.

1. Set up your space so that it feels comfortable and safe, using any objects you desire.

2. Sit or lie down, and start noticing your breath. As you inhale and exhale, pay attention to the rhythm of your breath. Notice the expansion and contraction. Say hello to your breath and your body.

3. With your eyes closed or gaze low, bring to mind a place that signals safety, peace, and calm to you—for example, somewhere in nature, or in your home or other inside space. Place yourself in this scene; are you sitting, standing up, lying down, etc.?

4. Focus on your sense of sight. What do you see? Look to your right, left, and behind you. Notice objects, colors, natural elements, and anything else in this safe space. State these things aloud.

5. Focus on your sense of smell. What scents is your nose picking up? (e.g., If you are by the ocean, perhaps you smell the seawater; if you are by the forest, perhaps you smell pine needles.)

6. Focus on your sense of sound. What sounds do you hear? (e.g., birds, waves, wind, chimes, or soft music)

7. Focus on your sense of taste. Lick your lips or move your tongue around in your mouth. What do you taste? (e.g., sea salt, a delicious fruit, a ripe berry, or perhaps nothing)

8. Focus on your sense of touch. Are your hands, feet, or other parts of your body in contact with something? What is it? (e.g., sand, leaves, wind, or a soft blanket)

9. Notice the temperature. Is it cool, warm, breezy, still, etc.?

10. Now take in all the sensory information at once, and pay attention to how your body is experiencing this moment. What are you noticing in your body? Is there perhaps an opening or a temperature

change? Just notice whatever may be emerging. If you don't notice anything yet, it's OK. The emergence of safety and calm in the body can take time.

11. When you are ready, orient yourself to your environment by noticing objects, colors, and textures.

Modifications

(1) Go to a physical place that feels peaceful, and journal what you notice with your five senses, or (2) If you have difficulty visualizing a safe place, look at a digital or printed photo of a beach, forest, or other peaceful image.

Journal Prompt

Describe your experience with this visualization. If you experienced any anxiety or discomfort around this exercise, journal about it to see if you can arrive at any insight of why this might be. As you repeat this exercise from time to time, keep track of your experience to see if there is any softening of the discomfort.

Internal Nurturing Figure

What You'll Need

- 20 to 30 minutes of uninterrupted time
- Art supplies such as paint or colored pencils and paper (optional)
- Journal and pen/pencil (or digital)

Childhood trauma can lead to issues with trust/betrayal, low self-esteem, self-judgment, self-regulation difficulties, and hostility toward self and others. Repeatedly not getting our needs met as kids makes it hard for us to understand and have compassion for the "needy parts" of ourselves. This exercise aims to help you cultivate an "imaginary" internal nurturing figure who is supportive, validating, and accepting so that you can start tuning in to this inner voice, gradually feeling more comfortable showing yourself and others compassion and understanding.

This exercise is influenced by attachment theory, which focuses on long-term bonds and relationships, and validates the value and profound impact of having a nurturing, supportive person in the healing process. It also draws from EMDR exercises, which use bilateral stimulation and eye movements to process trauma. This exercise isn't meant to downplay or dismiss any positive attachment figures from your childhood (i.e., healthy caregiver/parent-child relationships). Rather, it is meant to minimize the residue of traumatic memory and provide a strong foundation to help you regulate big emotions and process old wounds.

Note For this exercise, it's important not to use a real attachment figure (e.g., your mom, aunt, uncle, dad). To create positive associations from a blank slate, this figure should be someone you've never interacted with. This may feel unnatural or uncomfortable at first. It's OK if it takes time to develop and get used to this internal nurturing figure.

1. Sit comfortably with your journal in your calm, quiet space, and think about a nurturing, caring, and supportive person. This is not someone you know personally—for example, it may be a character from a book, movie, or TV show, or perhaps it is an ancestor or someone completely made up.

2. Start jotting down information about this person in your journal. If it's helpful, you can borrow qualities from fictional characters like Danny Tanner, the dad on *Full House,* or Clair Huxtable, the mom on *The Cosby Show.* What about them is warm and nurturing? What tone do they use when they speak? How do they make the people around them feel secure, respected, and at ease? Find words that describe the characteristics of this nurturing figure (e.g., supportive, understanding, thoughtful, calm, regulated, wise).

3. If you'd like to give physical characteristics to your nurturing figure, feel free to draw or paint what you see in your imagination or just describe it in your journal.

4. When you have a good idea of who this person is, close your eyes or gaze down. Focus your awareness on your body and the rhythm of your breath.

5. Bring your nurturing figure to mind. Imagine this figure sensing your presence and greeting you with delight. Notice how their gestures and words give you permission and space to be just as you are. Soak in their acceptance and understanding, and take note of how your body responds to their presence.

6. When you are ready, orient yourself to your environment by noticing objects, colors, and textures.

Journal Prompt

Describe your experience with this exercise. What thoughts and feelings emerged? Was any part of the exercise uncomfortable? Why or why not? Did you have an urge or impulse for the imaginary figure to say something hurtful or rejecting? If that was your experience, it's OK; just notice it and release it. Cultivating a nurturing figure without a direct experience of nurturing takes time.

Body Rhythm and Sensation Awareness

What You'll Need

- 20 to 30 minutes of uninterrupted time
- A rhythm object that expands and contracts, such as a Hoberman sphere, Slinky, stress/tension ball, or slime
- A cold object such as an ice pack
- A warm/hot object such as a heating pad
- Journal and pen/pencil (or digital)

This exercise helps you strengthen the relationship between your mind and body. You'll explore how your body holds information and how it communicates with you and your environment. You'll also start developing descriptive language to describe your internal experience.

As you've learned, trauma can become ingrained in the tissues of our body, manifesting as body sensations, constrictions, aches and pains, and/or areas of numbness and disconnection. This exercise draws from the work of Dr. Peter Levine, the founder of Somatic Experiencing® International, and Dr. Pat Ogden, the founder of Sensorimotor Psychotherapy Institute. Somatic Experiencing (SE™) and the Sensorimotor Psychotherapy method involve therapeutic exercises that engage the body in the treatment and healing of trauma for mental and emotional wellness.

It's common to feel detached and disconnected from ourselves as a result of going through trauma. This protective defense mechanism attempts to shield us from more pain and hurt, and while it serves a purpose, it also inhibits us from connecting to, expressing, and releasing the full range of our emotions. Bringing discovery, curiosity, and awareness to your body sensations and rhythms helps you integrate all parts of yourself and experiences into your whole being. As you do, you can start moving past traumatic childhood experiences and begin responding to triggers from a more integrated, balanced state.

Note There is no right or wrong way to practice increasing your awareness around your body sensations. Nor is there a right or wrong way to experience the progression/sequencing of sensations, your relationship to those sensations, and the meaning you make of them. You are gathering this information to get to know yourself and what happens for you. This is your gold nugget, not only to be able to describe your experiences and reactions but also to become OK with whatever is happening for you.

Instructions

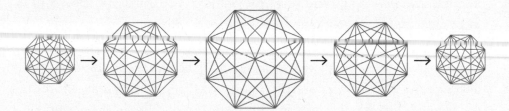

1. Stand or sit comfortably in your calm, quiet space, holding your rhythm object. Stretch it out and then contract it a few times to get a feel for it.

2. Now, allow the expansion and contraction of the object to mirror the rhythm of your breath. Alternate between your breath following the object and the object following your breath.

3. Inhale as you expand the object, noticing the expansion in your chest and belly. Exhale as you contract the object, noticing the collapse in your chest and belly. Become aware of other parts of your body that are also influenced by the expansion and contraction. Notice how the contraction must follow the expansion and vice versa; too much expansion without contraction cannot exist.

4. Place the rhythm object aside, and select either the warm or cold object for more awareness around body sensation.

5. Hold this temperature object in your hand. Notice how it feels. Look at the Somatic Feel Wheel at the end of this exercise to help you describe the sensations in your hand. How do you feel toward the sensation? Is there an urge or impulse to endure it? Is there a reaction to get rid of it? What happens if you ignore it? Just notice your reaction and observe the sensations.

6. Don't force yourself to hold the object, but do notice if you have a strong urge to "beat the sensation" or power through it. Perhaps you feel annoyed or are triggered by the temperature change. Again, just notice. You do not have to hold this object for very long to notice your reaction and observe the sensations in your body. Whatever you experience is valuable information.

7. Repeat this process with the other temperature object.

Modification

If using temperature objects feels too overwhelming, stick to just the rhythm object. You can also do this activity with a friend and share your experiences.

The Somatic Feel Wheel

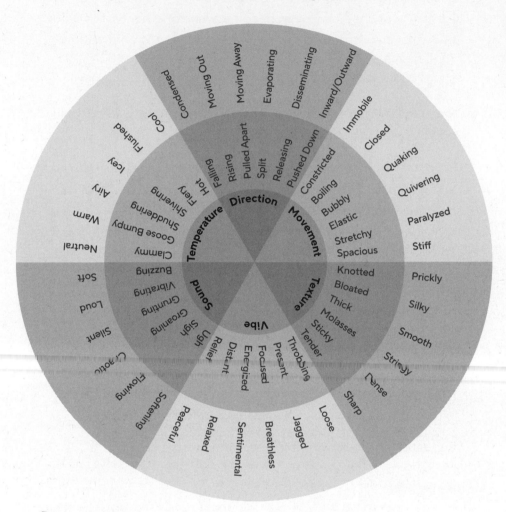

Journal Prompt

Describe what this exercise was like for you—first with the rhythm object and then with the temperature objects. What sensations in your body did you become aware of? What impulses or urges might have risen to the surface? What do those impulses or urges mean to you? Was there anything you experienced that surprised or embarrassed you? Jot down any emotions that emerged throughout this process.

The Container

What You'll Need

- 15 to 20 minutes of uninterrupted time
- Objects to serve as physical boundaries such as rocks, candles, or pillows (optional)
- Objects that represent safety and calm (optional)
- Journal and pen/pencil (or digital)

This exercise helps you develop a sense of containment for overwhelming or intense emotions by creating a sense of boundary (i.e., a container) using your imagination. This container is a safe and valuable place that enables you to hold memories or emotions when you are at risk of being overwhelmed or emotionally flooded by them.

Placing distressing memories or emotions in your container helps you return to your "window of tolerance" (see the graphic on the next page). This is your internal bandwidth for staying grounded, connected, and able to hold distressing emotions without feeling shut down, retraumatized, or dissociated. Outside your window of tolerance, it's difficult to cope and manage. When feeling overwhelmed, flooded, or triggered, you either ascend into a state of hyperarousal, which is when the body wants to fight or run away, or you may descend into a state of hypoarousal, which is when the body wants to freeze or shut down. When you are within your window of tolerance, however, you're able to learn, heal, and grow.

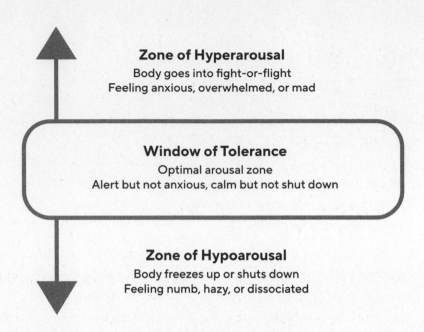

Zone of Hyperarousal
Body goes into fight-or-flight
Feeling anxious, overwhelmed, or mad

Window of Tolerance
Optimal arousal zone
Alert but not anxious, calm but not shut down

Zone of Hypoarousal
Body freezes up or shuts down
Feeling numb, hazy, or dissociated

Note This container is a safe, valuable place where you can store important information that you can later use to learn, heal, and grow. This exercise is not intended to invalidate, repress, or get rid of anything that's too distressing. Conversely, the idea is to strengthen your awareness of when you are bumping up against your boundaries and are about to exit (or have exited) your window of tolerance. This awareness enables you to guide your mind and body back to a place of safety and calm using this tool.

Instructions

1. Set up your space with any objects desired for comfort/safety as well as to represent boundaries. Sit or lie in a comfortable position, and close your eyes or gaze down.

2. Bring to mind an image of a container that holds something of great value, such as a treasure chest or fenced garden. Imagine its color(s), shape, and size.

3. When you have an image of this container in your mind, visualize placing inside it all the distressing feelings or memories you do not have capacity to hold right now.

4. Take your time visualizing storing away these feelings or memories, reminding yourself as you do so that you aren't locking them away with the intent to ignore them or disregard them. Rather, you are keeping them safe and protected for later engagement while also honoring the pacing of your internal system and acknowledging your limitations.

5. Offer yourself gratitude for guarding these emotions and memories, securing them until there is more time, space, or resources to hold or unpack them.

6. When you are ready, orient yourself to your environment by noticing objects, colors, and textures.

Journal Prompt

Reflect on your association with the image you used in this exercise. How did it feel to put certain feelings or memories aside for now?

Chapter 4

External Support for Healing Work

External support is essential for trauma healing work. Various therapies such as attachment-based therapy, concepts such as co-regulation, and healing practices such as nature therapy acknowledge that we are not separate from our outer experiences and social environments. They give us practical tools to interact with the reality of the world around us.

As you know, trauma is rarely an isolated internal event. It is usually the result of a distressing external experience that happens to us, which we then internalize and manifest through various symptoms. Therefore, building, reframing, and reclaiming our external environment can transform our environment from a place associated with discomfort into a resource of safety and connection. What's more, as we begin to heal internally, the healing radiates and impacts what's outside of us. We begin to desire, advocate, and create an external environment that matches our need for safety and connection. Equipped with the ability to ground ourselves both internally and externally, we can counteract moments of internal or external distress with the ability to shift and find safety on the opposite side of the coin.

5-4-3-2-1 Grounding Technique

What You'll Need

- 15 to 30 minutes of uninterrupted time
- Journal and pen/pencil (or digital)

We've all experienced moments when our mind becomes overly preoccupied with a thought that consequently leads us to disconnect from the world. Similarly, many of us have experienced sensations in our bodies that consume all our attention. On a spectrum from worrisome thoughts to panic attacks, these experiences can be debilitating, anxiety-provoking, and overwhelming to the point that we struggle to function.

The 5-4-3-2-1 Grounding Technique offers an excellent tool for supporting yourself when you feel overwhelmed, disconnected, internally preoccupied, dissociated, emotionally dysregulated, anxious, and/or triggered. You'll learn how to ground yourself and shift from internal or physical rumination to external awareness, where you are better able to identify safety in moments of distress. By focusing on your five senses one at a time, you reorient yourself to your environment, thereby increasing your awareness of the present moment. This helps you find tangible ways to shift out of an upsetting state. The overall objective is to ground yourself during moments of internal or physical overstimulation.

Note If you have difficulty engaging with a particular sense, just skip it and focus on the other senses. You can also get creative with your senses; for example, by identifying something you hear inside *and* something you can hear outside. When practicing this exercise, you can place objects in your environment to grab your attention and enhance your senses—a lit candle, for instance, that engages your sense of sight *and* smell.

Instructions

1. Sit or lie with your eyes open in your calm, quiet space. Take a deep breath, and slowly begin to scan your environment.

2. Identify and name five things you can see. Take a deep breath.

3. Identify and name four things you can feel or touch. Perhaps notice your feet on the ground, your body against the chair, your skin against your clothing. Take a deep breath.

4. Identify and name three things you can hear. Notice the subtle and loud sounds in your environment. Take a deep breath.

5. Identify and name two things you can smell. Feel free to move close to objects that may increase your ability to smell. Take a deep breath.

6. Name one thing you can taste. Feel free to drink a glass of water or take a bite of something small. Notice the taste. Take a deep breath.

7. Notice how present you are in your environment.

Journal Prompt

Describe your experience of noticing each of your five senses. Did you have difficulty engaging with any particular sense? Explore why that might be. How might this exercise be helpful to you in the ordinary course of the day?

Daily Rituals for Security and Stability

What You'll Need

- 15 minutes of uninterrupted time (three times a day)
- Journal and pen/pencil (or digital)

The brain loves to predict and quickly identify patterns to ensure our safety; it's basically a prediction and repetition machine that wants to ensure that the expected patterns can be completed successfully. Therefore, it scans the environment to assess for anything threatening or out of the ordinary that might disrupt the pattern. When a threat does occur, even if it's small, the body sends out an alert (an anxious reaction) to inform you that something's wrong and you must get to safety. If a threat does not occur, the brain feels safe and the body remains calm.

Engaging in rituals that promote safety, calmness, connection, and compassion is comforting to your mind and body. Your brain will detect a pattern of you showing up for yourself to meet your needs, leading to a sense of stability and security in your daily life. Establishing a consistent daily practice, which this exercise will guide you through, will help you make a habit of showing up for yourself, which is an essential aspect of self-healing.

Note Be as creative as you want with these daily practices. Expand, substitute, or create new rituals that you feel more of a connection to. The overall goal is to develop a calming pattern of nurturing yourself throughout the day that you—and your brain—can rely on. The key to any ritual is to be mindful and aware of what you are doing.

Morning Ritual: Intention-Setting

1. Settle down with your journal in your calm, quiet space, and tune in to your senses to bring you into the present moment.

2. Take a deep breath, and think of what you want to feel, achieve, experience, or learn today. As these thoughts come to mind, mindfully write them down. Notice any feelings, thoughts, and sensations in your body without responding to them; just affirm that part of you is desiring this thing today.

3. Once you've written down as many desires as you can think of, take a deep breath. Look at your list and choose three to create an intention around. Share your intentions with yourself by mindfully saying aloud, "Today my intention is to (*fill in the blank*)." Feel your body connecting with those words. Revisit your intentions throughout the day, as desired.

Afternoon Ritual: Mindful Walking

1. Locate a place where you can go for an afternoon walk each day—five minutes one way and five minutes back, at a slow pace. This place might be in your neighborhood, at a park, along the shore, outside your place of work, etc.

2. As you prepare to set out for your walk, stand firmly and take a deep breath. Notice your feet on the ground and your legs holding your body.

3. As you take your first, slow step, notice your leg lifting and the sole of your foot touching the ground. Repeat with your other foot and leg. Notice each step and how your feet engage with the ground beneath you.

4. Mindfully notice all the physical sensations and movements of your body as you walk—your neck and shoulders, your arms and hands, your chest and stomach, your hips and legs, all the way down to your feet. If your thoughts wander or something in the environment grabs your attention, notice it without judgment, take a deep breath, and shift your attention back to the physical sensations connected to each step.

5. Once you reach the halfway point, turn around and continue walking mindfully until you reach your destination. Once there, take a deep breath and orient yourself to your environment by engaging your five senses.

Evening Ritual: Leaves on a Stream

1. Sit or lie in your calm, quiet space (play soothing music, if desired). Take a deep breath, and close your eyes or gaze down. Remind yourself to acknowledge thoughts, body sensations, and your overall self without judgment. The goal is just to observe and notice.

2. Now imagine yourself sitting on a bench looking at a gently flowing stream with leaves slowly floating down the stream. Take some time to make the visual more palpable by including your five senses. What are you seeing, touching, hearing, smelling, and tasting?

3. Notice any thoughts you may be having at this moment. It could be a thought, a worry, or a memory you are replaying in your mind; just notice it and pause. Now imagine placing this thought on top of a leaf and watching it float down the stream.

4. Notice any feelings that may be surfacing at this time (e.g., sadness, restlessness, or even boredom); just notice the feeling and pause. Now imagine placing the feeling on a leaf and watching it float down the stream.

5. Notice any body sensations. Whether pleasant, unpleasant, or neutral, just notice it and pause. Now imagine placing the body sensation on a leaf and watching it float down the stream.

6. Continue for as long as you want, placing thoughts, feelings, and/or body sensations on a leaf and slowly watching each one float down the stream.

7. When you are ready, take a deep breath and orient yourself to your environment by engaging your five senses.

Journal Prompt

Describe your experience with each ritual. Are you likely to do them daily? Why or why not? What other rituals might you want to try in place of one or more of these? Would you like to try yoga, meditation, stretching, praying, another spiritual practice, or something else? Reflect on how one or more of these practices might help you on your healing journey.

Holding Your Object of Safety

- 15 to 30 minutes of uninterrupted time
- Journal and pen/pencil (or digital)
- A stuffed animal or other object of safety such as a pet, toy, ball, or blanket, preferably associated with a positive childhood memory

In this exercise, you will learn to connect with your inner child by using a stuffed animal or other safety object to practice reparenting skills and posture. In a 2012 journal article that examined animals as attachment objects, researchers M. Rose Barlow and colleagues found that both stuffed animals and live animals can be used in therapy to help patients feel and express their emotions and experience a sense of unconditional support while feeling grounded. This creates a sense of connection, security, and comfort, which as we know, is one of the best ways to reduce stress and anxiety. When we experience feelings of rejection, alienation, and/or abandonment, holding a stuffed animal or another object of safety can help ground us and reduce feelings of loneliness.

Many people associate stuffed animals with childhood. Taking care of a stuffed animal or other object of safety the way you want to be taken care of begins the process of nurturing your inner child. When you learn how to engage, soothe, and show up for your inner child in a tangible way, you create the opportunity to meet needs that went unmet for you as a child while expressing and experiencing associated emotions in the present.

British pediatrician and psychoanalyst Donald Winnicott made a distinction between "handling" and "holding" in relation to how a parent engages their child. *Handling* refers to the parent's meeting the physical needs of the child (e.g., providing food, clothing, and shelter), whereas *holding* refers to the parent's meeting the child's emotional needs (e.g., being present, engaged, and supportive; providing positive physical touch). In addition, *holding* means to create an emotional containment for the child to feel safe enough to express their feelings and thoughts, as well as their overall self. This exercise puts Winnicott's concept of holding into practice. You will explore giving and receiving gentle physical support, be it a simple touch or holding that leads you to an experience of safe emotional bonding.

Note Feel free to hold your object of safety to comfort yourself any time you feel overwhelmed or dysregulated. While using an object of safety similar to one you had as a child is beneficial for this exercise, you can use any object of safety that feels soothing to hold.

Instructions

1. Sit in your calm, quiet space and relax with your object of safety in a way that feels comfortable and safe. Softly observe your surroundings, noticing your body and how it feels as your bottom and legs rest against your seat.

2. Hold your object of safety, and slowly observe its details and dimensions. Gently feel its texture, temperature, and weight.

3. Close your eyes or gaze down and draw your memory back to a pleasant or neutral time during your childhood when you were holding an object of safety. If an unpleasant memory arises, acknowledge the memory and imagine it floating out of your awareness. Look at these exercise prompts for stability.

4. As the pleasant or neutral memory comes, notice your inner child's environment—the sounds, smells, and what you were touching. Notice your object of safety in your inner child's hands.

5. Notice the emotions and body sensations that are coming up for you now.

6. Sit with the feelings and the memory for one or two minutes while holding your object of safety. Whenever you feel comfortable, slowly open or raise your eyes, letting them adjust to the light in the room.

7. Continue to hold your object of safety and again feel its texture, temperature, and weight in a gentle manner. Hold your object of safety for as long as you like.

Journal Prompt

Reflect on the childhood memory associated with your object of safety. What was it like seeing your younger self in a calm manner holding their object of safety? What were the feelings and body sensations that came up for you? When might be a good time for you to hold your object of safety?

Exploring External Relationships and Attachments

What You'll Need

- 20 to 60 minutes of uninterrupted time
- Journal and pen/pencil (or digital)

We all generally have moments during childhood when we connect, feel safe, and build bonds with others (such as a parent, grandparent, sibling, friend, or teacher)—even if those moments are small. These positive attachments (supportive relationships) make us feel comfortable, less guarded, and safe enough to express ourselves. As children, we internalize how these people connect and communicate acceptance, which adds to our development of a healthy sense of self-worth.

During childhood, it's imperative to have supportive relationships in moments when we felt distressed in order to heal from that distress. This is because these supportive relationships provide affirmation, approval, and safety, which are directly opposed to shame and other feelings connected to trauma. Let's say you were bullied in school when you were ten years old. Did you have someone who made you feel safe and connected in their presence despite the bullying at school? Perhaps a friend, parent, family member, or teacher? While your relationship with that person may have felt natural and perhaps even insignificant, in retrospect it provided you with a positive emotional attachment in which your boundaries were respected and you experienced a sense of closeness, which was essential to your well-being at the time.

The concept of attachment is at the root of many types of therapy. A therapist may use relational attachment theory to help a client counteract and heal feelings and symptoms of shame, trauma, anxiety, etc. by meeting those issues with acceptance, warmth, trust, and security, which are the foundation of positive attachments and the opposite of what was experienced in the past. Such interactions, when repeated and remembered, lead to a secure attachment, which helps the client learn to feel safe when getting close to others, and create healthy boundaries.

In this exercise, you'll explore positive and negative attachments during three different points of your childhood by creating an eco-map, which is basically a visual, therapeutic tool to explore relationships, how they impacted you, and any residues you may still carry from them. As you do this exercise, pay close attention to what feelings arise and how your body responds to each person's name. Do they make you feel safe, excited, and calm? Do they make you feel anxious, fearful, distrustful, rejected, or abandoned? Do you shut down emotionally—a part of you wants to dismiss your feelings or is unwilling to tap into your emotions? Gaining insight into these reactions can help you identify areas of your life that you can affirm, improve, and/or change.

Note Gaining awareness of how past relationships impacted you and how you may still be responding to those relationships is critical to your healing. While we encourage you to identify these relationships and thoroughly reflect on them, if one of these relationships feels too stressful to reflect on, identify one that's less emotionally stimulating at first.

Instructions

1. Sit in your calm, quiet space with your journal and ground yourself by engaging your five senses. What can you see, touch, smell, hear, and/or taste?

2. When ready, create the following eco-map in your journal, filling in your reflections row by row. Take your time.

Put your pen down and take a deep breath. Notice and observe your body sensations and feelings connected to each name.

3. Ground yourself again by engaging your five senses, and then close your eyes or gaze down.

4. Imagine a real or fictional nurturing figure (this can be the one you identified in the exercise on page 54). Hold the image of this nurturing figure in your mind. What are the nurturing traits connected to this person? How would this person provide you with comfort, support, and understanding?

5. Notice and observe your body sensations and feelings as you hold the image of this person and their nurturing traits in mind.

6. When ready, orient yourself to your environment by engaging your five senses once again.

Positive and Negative Attachment Eco-Map

AGE OR PERIOD OF LIFE	E.G., SIX YEARS OLD OR ELEMENTARY SCHOOL	E.G., TWELVE YEARS OLD OR MIDDLE SCHOOL	E.G., SIXTEEN YEARS OLD, TEEN YEARS, OR HIGH SCHOOL
NAME OF POSITIVE FIGURE			
What is/was significant about this person?			
How did this person make you feel?			
What is/was different about them?			
What response did they evoke from you?			
Who did you become around them?			

AGE OR PERIOD OF LIFE	E.G., SIX YEARS OLD OR ELEMENTARY SCHOOL	E.G., TWELVE YEARS OLD OR MIDDLE SCHOOL	E.G., SIXTEEN YEARS OLD, TEEN YEARS, OR HIGH SCHOOL
NAME OF NEGATIVE OR STRESSFUL FIGURE			
What was painful about the relationship with this person?			
What was your experience of being understood or heard by this person?			

Journal Prompt

Reflect on positive relationships during your childhood. How did they positively impact you? Now, reflect on the nurturing figure you chose for the second part of the exercise. Why did you choose this person? What qualities of theirs do you value? Describe the feelings and sensations that came up for you during any or all parts of this exercise.

Grounding with Nature

What You'll Need

- 15 to 30 minutes of uninterrupted time
- An outdoor space
- Journal and pen/pencil (or digital)

"We are part of the earth and the earth is a part of us" is an indigenous proverb that gets to the essence of the inseparable interlinkage we humans have with the earth. In this nature grounding exercise, you will connect your physical body to the earth and vice versa. You will create moments of mindfulness where you join the earth to create an inner sense of balance and safety.

Nature grounding practices have benefited humans for millennia; many ancient cultures viewed grounding/earthing as a healing and spiritual practice. Dr. Stephen Sinatra, a cardiologist, brought the concept of earthing/grounding to the university lab and concluded from his research that grounding/earthing can lead to a reduction in anxiety, stress, trauma-related symptoms, and inflammation. Despite these benefits, we as humans have strayed away from engaging with the earth around us. We once were people who based our whole existence on the way we interacted with the earth.

Nature grounding can be as simple as taking the time to go outside and notice the natural air and trees in your neighborhood, mindfully walking barefooted on grass, going for a mindful hike, or running your hands through flowing water or sand. Overall, nature grounding helps you withdraw from the daily hustle and bustle of society. It grounds your body in nature's beauty and calms your nervous system.

Note Nature grounding is different from mindful walking (where the focus is more on engaging with your body); here you are using your external environment to ground you.

Instructions

1. Locate a place where you can go for a walk in nature for at least 10 minutes. As you prepare to set out for your walk, take a deep breath.

2. Intentionally engage your five senses:

   - Notice what you see around you. What particularly captures your attention? Which colors pop out at you?

   - Notice what you are touching. Feel your feet on the ground. Are you holding something? Can you reach out and touch something?

   - Notice the sounds around you. Can you differentiate between the sounds? How does each sound make your body feel?

   - What are the smells? Does any particular smell capture your attention?

   - What, if anything, do you taste? Is there something you can bring to your mouth, such as water?

3. Now, slowly take your first few steps, noticing the earth beneath your feet. As you walk farther, mindfully notice the weather and how your body is responding to the temperature.

4. Begin to identify small markers (such as a tree, flower, stone, water, or a view). Allow yourself to hold space and reverence for this marker. As you do so, bring your awareness to your senses. What do you notice when you look at the marker? Can you touch it? How does it feel? What does it smell like? Are there any sounds or tastes connected to the marker?

5. Take a mindful "snapshot" of your marker. Continue to look at it for at least 30 seconds, observing and letting your memory soak in every detail.

6. Continue walking and slowing down as often as you'd like to notice markers in nature. Repeat steps 4 and 5 for each marker you encounter until you return to your starting point.

Modifications

If going outside isn't possible right now, you can invite nature inside (for example, hold rocks, water plants, use essential oils, and eat organic food or beverages with mindfulness). If you are walking in a cityscape, you can look up to the sky and the clouds, while also acknowledging the architecture, energy, or objects that make you feel good. You can also simply hold reverence for parts of the world that remind you of the earth.

Journal Prompt

Reflect on your walk. What in nature stuck out to you? How did your body respond to the nature markers? Describe in detail some of the mindful "snapshots" you took. What were the feelings and body sensations that came up for you during this exercise?

Part Three

Tending Your Wounds

Chapter 5

Rewiring the Survival Mind

Living with the impact of trauma can feel overwhelming and hopeless at times, especially when the survival brain (the part that's always on the lookout for threats) keeps us in a chronic state of fight, flight, or freeze. Engaging in trauma healing work can help rewire our survival mind (aka the lizard brain) to shift out of this fight, flight, or shutdown pattern into a more regulated state.

When we learn to hold space for ourselves (that is, to be present to our internal experience without judgment), to validate some of our most wounded experiences, and to be in a new relationship with our pain, we create the potential for new neural pathways to be formed. With this "rewiring," a new internal relationship with ourselves takes shape, which outwardly births a new relationship with our environment. This cultivates self-compassion, curiosity, confidence, and increased emotional regulation.

The first two exercises in this chapter draw from the Internal Family Systems Model (IFS), which was developed by Richard C. Schwartz, PhD. This modality embraces the idea that we each have a core self in the "driver's seat" along with an internal system of protective and wounded inner parts that are established during childhood, and that each part has its own memories, emotions, and coping mechanisms. The 2015 Pixar movie *Inside Out* put a wonderful spin on this concept; it's a good movie to watch to get an idea for how the different parts of ourselves might interact. Like the characters in the movie, our different parts may have conflicting needs, beliefs, and/or desires. Likely you've experienced a time when "part of you" wanted to go out with your friends while another "part of you" wanted to stay home and be alone. Both parts are valid and worthy of getting to know, understand, and heal; this is true for *all* parts of you. IFS-based and related exercises in which you examine different aspects of yourself can help you develop the tools to do this.

Acknowledging Your Protective Parts

What You'll Need

- 20 to 30 minutes of uninterrupted time
- Journal and pen/pencil (or digital)
- Colored pencils or markers and drawing paper (optional)

This IFS-based exercise introduces you to the concept of "protective parts"—the parts of you that want to protect you from emotional pain. It will give you an opportunity to explore and get to know these parts, which you may not yet be aware of. Some protective parts are more reactive in how they protect you from pain (e.g., numbing, dissociating, bingeing, or self-harm), while other protective parts try to head off potential pain (e.g., perfectionism, controlling, or overworking). *All* these parts want to shield you from pain, and work very hard to do so, even if their tactics aren't always very effective. Learning to identify your protective parts can influence the way you relate to yourself and your behaviors, leading to increased happiness and inner harmony.

The purpose of this exercise is to increase awareness around body sensations related to sensing threats and how your body stores fear, worry, and/or anxiety. You'll begin to explore the power not only of internal awareness but also of "being with" parts of yourself as opposed to "being in" these parts of yourself. For example, let's say you're angry and disappointed with a friend who didn't include you in a gathering. Instead of "being in" those emotions, you take a breather and try to understand why some parts of you feel so angry and disappointed by your friend's behavior. This "being with" the anger and disappointment and trying to understand these emotions engages a different part of your brain—an inner audience, so to speak—that understands and validates how you feel.

Note An important part of this exercise is to acknowledge your protective parts and decide to what extent you want to explore your internal system with curiosity. Therefore, this exercise includes a suggestion to pause if you feel ungrounded as well as a suggestion to go deeper if you feel open and curious.

Instructions

1. Sit in your calm, quiet space with your journal handy. Draw an outline of a body on a fresh page in your journal or on drawing paper to serve as an external map of your internal parts.

2. Reflect on ways you protect yourself from feeling pain as well as ways you avoid pain. Also reflect on the parts that hold the pain. In IFS terminology, these are your "Protectors." Protective parts can show up as perfectionism, being controlling, overworking, numbing out, isolating, stonewalling, getting defensive, arguing, having to prove your worth, and so on. Choose one of these Protectors to work with.

3. Once you have selected the protective part, see if you can locate this part of you in or around your body. Where do you sense it? Place a mark on the outline of the body indicating where this part of you resides.

4. Notice the energy of this part—for example, is it light, heavy, wispy, constricted, smooth, rough, bumpy, moving, vibrating? You can color in and draw on this part of the outline in a way that represents these descriptions, if you'd like. If you can't identify these types of qualities, think of a fictional character, image, or other visual aid to represent the energy of this Protector.

5. Continue to explore this part. What does it want you to know? How does it communicate with you? Stay in the observational state of just noticing what emerges.

6. If you are struggling to stay grounded, pause and regroup. Perhaps take a break or do the 5-4-3-2-1 Grounding Technique on page 66. If you can hold openhearted curiosity, ask about the ways this part of you tries to protect yourself. Optionally, ask what it is trying to protect you from. What does it *not* want you to experience? If anything emerges, acknowledge and offer gratitude to this part for all its efforts to protect you.

7. Feel free to engage further by journaling and/or doing an art project to continue to explore and get to know this part of yourself.

8. When you're ready to end the activity, offer this part of you gratitude for showing up and being seen. Take three to four deep breaths to settle your system. Tune in to notice if you felt an energy shift.

Journal Prompt

Describe what this exercise was like for you. Was it challenging to observe one of your Protectors? Why or why not? Did you have any urges or impulses that emerged while you were exploring this part of yourself?

Befriending Your Many Parts

What You'll Need

- 20 to 40 minutes of uninterrupted time
- Drawing paper or poster board (optional)
- Colored pencils or markers (optional)
- Journal and pen/pencil (or digital)

In this IFS-based exercise, you'll begin considering the complexities of what it means to be human by exploring how seemingly contradictory needs and emotions (e.g., longing and resistance; sadness and joy) can coexist. You'll learn how to hear stories from multiple parts of yourself to get a better understanding of how they influence your responses and beliefs as well as what each part may need to feel more supported.

Making an effort to befriend the various parts of yourself helps regulate and restore harmony to your system. You'll begin by extending a hand in friendship to parts of yourself that you can more easily identify. Externalizing these parts helps you see that, yes, they are part of you, but not *all* of you. This gives you the distance you need to practice observing, noticing, and fostering a sense of curiosity, which will help you better regulate your emotions and responses down the road.

Note It's OK to be honest with yourself about your starting point. If you are unable to cultivate any curiosity or nonjudgment toward a part of you, that's a sign that you need to regroup. Go back to the exercises in chapters 3 and 4 to further develop your inner and external resources.

1. Sit in your calm, quiet space. Set an intention to embody the grounded qualities of self-compassion, patience, and curiosity. Place any art supplies you are using nearby or simply do this exercise in your journal. You can draw an outline of the body as you did in the previous exercise to help you map out your parts.

2. Think about parts of yourself you may already be familiar with. Sometimes parts can resemble emotions (e.g., the sad part and the fearful part). Other times, they can be more complex and take on specific functions (e.g., the self-sabotaging part, the people-pleasing part, the perfectionist part, the shy part, the high-achieving part, the strong part, and the critical part). From those parts, choose one that you feel some sense of gratitude for.

3. On your paper or poster board, start jotting down anything that comes into your awareness about this part. Include everything you already know, and then explore further. Do any images, shapes, colors, animals, and/or fictional characters come to mind that represent this part? If so, express it on paper or poster board—or describe it in your journal.

4. Does this part of you have beliefs or mantras that it frequently operates by? Some examples might be, "If I'm not perfect, I'm a failure" or "I need to muscle through this to reach my goal." Observe what comes up as you reflect on this, and write it down. Use different colors, block letters, small print—whatever seems suitable for those beliefs or mantras.

5. What is the energy or emotion of this part? Is there a particular vibe it gives off? Does it have texture? Is it frantic or panicking? Is it reserved or shut off? Jot it down or draw it.

6. Locate this part. Where does it show up in or around your body? Jot it down or draw it.

7. How do you feel toward this part of you? If you are feeling afraid or angry, go back a few steps and just focus on observing and noticing. If you are feeling curious or compassionate, move to the next step.

8. Imagine that you are taking this part of you out for coffee. During this get-together, you are giving it your full attention. You are learning to hold space for it, listen to it, and develop a friendship with it. Ask about its likes and dislikes. How would it feel for this part of you to be fully known, to be seen, to be understood? Draw or write anything that comes to you, or just put your supplies aside.

9. After you've spent some time together, thank this part for showing up and let it know that you're leaving and will return at another time. Orient yourself to your surroundings. Notice doors/exits, windows, colors, textures, and temperature as you return to the present moment.

Journal Prompt

What was it like for you to imagine developing a friendship with this part? How did it feel to spend time with it and to actively listen to what it had to say without any judgment?

Reflecting on Overwhelm and Disconnect

- 20 to 40 minutes of uninterrupted time
- Journal and pen/pencil (or digital)

In earlier chapters and exercises, we explored how the body's psychological response to a real or perceived threat or danger can override the logical/thinking brain and activate the stress response. Originally termed the fight-or-flight response by Walter Bradford Cannon in his 1915 book *Bodily Changes in Pain, Hunger, Fear and Rage,* the stress response continues to be better understood, and additional terms have been added for more clarification. For example, we've discussed the fight, flight, or freeze response in earlier parts of this book. Now, we will use a fourth term as well: fight, flight, freeze, or *fawn* response.

As you've learned, freeze is the body's inability to move or act against a threat. This looks like dissociation, feeling spacey, feeling numb, or feeling detached from yourself or your body. Having one's body autonomy, sense of agency, choice, and/or boundaries violated can trigger a freeze response. The fawn response, however, is an act of submission to pacify or avoid any type of conflict from emerging. Fawn responses can become automatic in cases of a highly controlled, abusive, or volatile environment. Fawn responses can also be a reflexive response due to harm or ruptures in early relationships that have not been repaired, usually over a prolonged period. The urge to submit comes from the fear of abandonment and losing connection to a person.

Both the freeze response and fawn response can cause a feeling of being stuck and/or overwhelmed. It can leave us feeling trapped and incapable of making decisions or moving forward. In this exercise, you'll learn to identify an oncoming freeze/fawn response and how to slow the process or stop the disconnection from happening.

Note If you become overwhelmed thinking about or participating in this exercise, slow down, regroup, and do some of the exercises in chapters 3 and 4 to strengthen your internal and external resources. You can also do this exercise with other qualities, such as procrastination or self-sabotage, which can also be how the freeze/fawn response shows up for some. If you chronically feel in a state of overwhelm and cannot imagine a time when you have not disconnected from that feeling, reflect on the intensity of the overwhelm and see if you notice a decrease.

Instructions

1. Sit in your calm, quiet space with your journal handy.

2. Bring to mind a memory of the last time you felt a sense of overwhelm or dread that led you to procrastinate, shut down, zone out, or get stuck that you would rate a 3 or 4 on a distress scale of 0 to 10, with 10 being the most distressing and 0 being not distressing at all. (You can work with higher ratings later.)

3. Try to recall steps or triggers that led to this feeling of overwhelm and jot them down in your journal. Reflect on these questions:

    -   When did you notice an increase of stress?

    -   How did the overwhelm show up in your body?

    -   Did you start to respond to the overwhelm before you shut down (e.g., talked more, increased activity, isolated, experienced shortness of breath)?

    -   Did you notice yourself becoming numb? If so, when did you become aware of the numbness? In which part of your body did you notice the numbness?

4. Now consider what happens once you feel maxed out or totally overwhelmed. Do you pull away from others? Cling to others? Seek reassurance? Disconnect from support and rely on yourself only? Write down anything that comes to mind.

5. Set an intention to remember this information. The more aware you are of your triggers and responses, the more you can step in and halt the spiral toward disconnect.

6. When you are ready, take a deep breath and orient yourself to your environment by engaging your five senses.

Journal Prompt

Describe what you would say or do to help another person get unstuck. What exercise would you encourage them to do? Why? What parts of your body feel stuck right now?

A Date with Loneliness

What You'll Need

- 45 to 60 minutes of uninterrupted time
- Journal and pen/pencil (or digital)

Being alone and feeling lonely can be two different experiences. Being alone can be a positive experience when there's a sense of wholeness and compassion for oneself and one's experiences, but when being alone feels emotionally painful, it is defined as loneliness. This exercise is intended to help you reframe your understanding, experience, and relationship to being alone and the feeling of loneliness.

When you explore what loneliness means to you and your history with it, you will gain a better understanding of how you have experienced loneliness in the past. You'll also be able to reframe how you engage with this feeling now. It may take time before you can tease out distressing experiences with *feeling* alone versus positive experiences with *being* alone. When there is a history of neglect, being alone can be triggering (and for good reason!). The survival mind (aka the lizard brain) tells our body that we must be in close contact with another person or we will die, thereby activating the fight, flight, or freeze response. While the goal is to be OK engaging with others on some occasions and being alone on others, take these steps slowly and cautiously to honor your survival mind, as it may require small spurts of being alone to feel the nurturing benefits.

Note The self-care activities suggested in this exercise can all be done in your home or in close proximity to it. However, you can also practice farther from home, such as in a bookstore. If this is what you choose, be in proximity to an exit, have your phone handy, and look for people to engage with if needed. This will help your survival mind settle down, knowing that being alone can be done in a safe, supportive way and in short spurts. Even if you are unable to tolerate being alone for very long, that's OK. Whatever time you do spend is a starting point and valuable. It's OK to simply acknowledge where you're at and take it from there.

Instructions

1. Sit in your calm, quiet space with your journal handy. Think about a self-care activity you can do by yourself that feels nurturing and safe. Some examples include soaking in a bath or taking a shower, stretching or yoga, and going for a walk outside.

2. Set your journal aside, and go engage in this activity for about 20 to 30 minutes, and then return to your space. Briefly reflect on this experience in your journal.

3. Now, name some experiences in your life when being alone was scary or triggering, jotting down whatever feels important to name; there is no need to unpack them or reexperience them.

4. From the experiences you named, choose one or two of these moments to explore. What happened around you that made you feel alone? What did you need in that time of loneliness? Practice offering comfort or responding with tenderness to the part of you experiencing that loneliness.

5. Now, try to identify any positive experiences you've had of being by yourself. If you can't think of any from your past, reflect on how any part of the self-care activity you engaged in earlier felt positive. If you've never experienced a positive experience of being alone, then just notice how you are responding to doing this exercise. Reflect on the current moment.

6. Close out this time by writing a note of gratitude to yourself for what you learned or experienced during this exercise.

Journal Prompt

Reflect on what your inner dialogue sounded like while doing this exercise. Was it critical? Supportive? Indifferent? Brainstorm what type of freedoms being alone could offer you (e.g., listen to loud music, comment aloud while watching TV, read for as long as you like, dance like nobody's watching, laugh at the top of your lungs).

Connecting to Your Roots

- 15 to 30 minutes of uninterrupted time
- Journal and pen/pencil (or digital)

Language is an integral part of our identity, shaping who we are and how we perceive the world. The mother tongue (i.e., the first language or dialect we were exposed to from birth) provides us with verbiage to connect feelings with words and gives us a way to describe and understand our initial associations. It helps shape and organize the way we see ourselves and sets the tone we use with ourselves. It also plays a huge role in the development of inner dialogues.

In this exercise, you'll identify the essence of your mother tongue and how it has impacted you. You'll also explore how language can be connected to different parts of yourself. Moreover, if you had to learn to code-switch (switch from one language or dialect to another), speak a different language, or navigate language from an outsider's perspective, this exercise can help you connect to the part that's often pushed to the back in favor of the dominant language. Speaking in our mother tongue essentially unlocks a part of our identity and memory that is deeply connected to our childhood and cultural roots.

Speaking a "different" language can also tap into different parts of ourselves and evoke different emotions. For example, we've worked with many clients who had a bilingual or code-switching upbringing. In moments when such a client might have difficulty communicating a thought or feeling from their childhood, we may encourage them to express it in their mother tongue. It does not matter if we understand it—using their mother tongue honors their original feeling and memory, which helps the client cultivate a greater authenticity, understanding, and connection to that part of their lives.

Note This exercise isn't only for folks from bilingual backgrounds or even a verbal language background (the sign-language community is welcome to explore mother tongue, too). This is more about exploring your relationship to communicating with others through body language and gestures, tonal cues, energies, facial expressions, and felt experiences (emotional responses) within your family of origin or from your caregivers.

Instructions

1. Sit in your calm, quiet space. Bring to mind an occasion from your childhood when your caretakers/family members were gathered and the overall mood was that the adults could be comfortable being themselves without reservation. Consider these questions:

    - What language is being spoken?

    - Are they using words, phrases, or informal language that is unique to a particular context or group of people?

    - What's the style, tone, or energy of the language?

    - Is the language inviting and open, captivating, proper, informal, lighthearted, passive-aggressive, harsh, aggressive, taboo, or something else?

2. It's not only the meaning of the words that are internalized during childhood but also the tones and feelings behind the language. What were the messages or what meaning did you make from the tones and feelings the adults used with you and others?

3. Outside the imagined scenario, explore the level of verbal aggression during your upbringing. How intense was the language at home? In what types of situations did the language become more aggressive?

4. What happens to your body when you think about the feelings connected to the language spoken in your childhood? Notice your body sensations. Does an image connected to your childhood language come to mind? If so, observe the image along with your feelings.

5. If you notice that parts of your body feel tight or constricted, slowly settle your body by taking deep breaths. Identify a part of your body that feels neutral or pleasant, and focus on that part as you take three deep breaths.

6. Now think about the language or style of speech your younger self deserved to hear. Think about the image of your younger self from earlier and imagine giving your younger self new language and affirmations.

7. Say three things that your younger self deserved to hear as a child. Notice how your body responds to the affirmations and new language. Validate these bodily responses.

8. When ready, orient yourself to your environment by engaging your five senses.

Modification

The mother tongue can be connected to a lot of trauma; if you find that reflecting on your childhood language is too overwhelming, think about your relationship to communicating in different environments and how language may impact your mood. Also, consider how forms of speech can stimulate a specific personality in you.

Journal Prompt

Describe the feelings most associated with the language spoken in your childhood home. What do you notice happens to your body when you think about your mother tongue? What style or tone of speech opens you up? What style or tone of speech shuts you down?

Chapter 6

Redeveloping Emotional Wellness

The National Institutes of Health defines "emotional wellness" as "the ability to successfully handle life's stresses and adapt to change and difficult times." To achieve emotional wellness, we must first have a relationship with our emotional self, which includes various parts of our personality as well as our energetic states—only then are we able to successfully manage and balance our emotions. The process of creating emotional wellness begins with becoming aware of, acknowledging, and exploring unprocessed memories and emotions—and ultimately releasing them.

When a specific emotion is taken out of context for the purpose of getting to know that emotion on a deeper level and exploring why it's showing up at this particular time, we can find unique ways to manage or release that emotion when it comes up. For example, getting to know anger on a deeper level gives us more of an understanding about why, in moments of anger, one person may shut down while another rages. It also helps us develop ways to harmoniously respond to the various upsetting emotions without repressing them. Additionally, getting to know emotions over time, as you will begin to do in this chapter, assists in establishing a relationship with them, which then allows you to regulate them. Going through this process is imperative in trauma healing work because you'll be more prepared to understand and manage your emotional experiences and bodily reactions in the face of stressors and triggers.

Riding the Polyvagal "Elevator"

What You'll Need

- 15 to 20 minutes of uninterrupted time
- Journal and pen/pencil (or digital)

The polyvagal theory, developed by Dr. Stephen Porges, is a framework for our autonomic nervous system. This theory proposes that we have three unique responses to our environment, especially in moments of stress: (1) social engagement (the ventral vagal system), (2) fight or flight (the sympathetic system), and (3) freeze, or shutdown (the dorsal vagal system). This theory helps us better understand the connection between the body and mind and increases our awareness of instances in which we feel safe and secure and moments when we feel either dysregulated (fight or flight) or emotionally shut down (freeze).

This exercise helps you track and regulate your nervous system while gaining knowledge of how these three systems are linked. You'll better understand how trauma impacts your nervous system and how safety and social engagement can help you manage your physical and emotional state. To clarify, think of your autonomic nervous system as a three-story building:

- **Top floor:** This is the social engagement floor. Here, you feel safe and connected to others, your body feels calm and at ease, and you can effectively express thoughts and feelings.
- **Middle floor:** This is the fight-or-flight floor. Here, your body and mind are sensing some type of danger; you are on high alert, filled with energy to either fight or run from the perceived danger.
- **Bottom floor:** This is the freeze/shutdown floor. You sense danger, but your body becomes immobile, or you emotionally shut down and disconnect.

The objective of this exercise is to get to know when you feel physically/emotionally elevated as well as when you feel emotionally/physically immobile and disconnected. The goal then is to be able to recognize each state and move yourself toward social engagement.

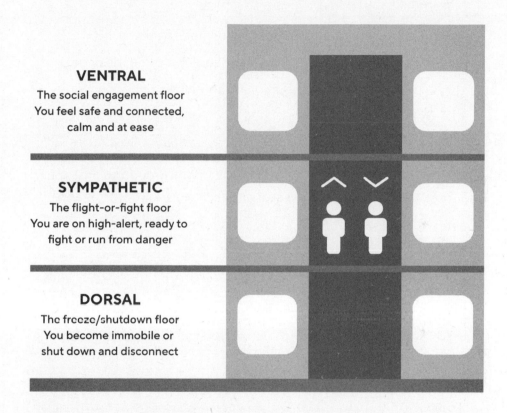

VENTRAL
The social engagement floor
You feel safe and connected, calm and at ease

SYMPATHETIC
The flight-or-fight floor
You are on high-alert, ready to fight or run from danger

DORSAL
The freeze/shutdown floor
You become immobile or shut down and disconnect

Note This exercise helps you recognize and connect to each state of the autonomic nervous system. It can help you identify moments when you might benefit from the support of a family member, friend, or professional, or perhaps from doing a relaxing activity, going someplace calming and affirming, or engaging with a pet. Think about people, places, things, and activities that emotionally settle you so you can seek support when needed.

1. Sit in your calm, quiet space. Prepare yourself with three recent memories that have an intensity level of about 3 or 4 on a distress scale of 0 to 10, with 0 being not distressing at all and 10 being extremely distressing:

   a. a time when you felt safe and connected to others,

   b. a time when you felt an impulse to confront someone or get away,

   c. a time where you felt emotionally shut down or disconnected from others.

   Write them in your journal if that would be helpful.

2. Take a deep breath, notice the contact of the ground against your feet, the contact of your seat against a chair, and your arms and hands making contact with a surface. Practice noticing sensations, contact, pressure, and texture on/in your body.

3. Close your eyes or gaze down, and imagine a three-story building. Slowly enter the building. As you enter the bottom floor, notice that there's an elevator that will take you to the second floor. Look back toward the exit and remind yourself you can exit at any time if you feel too overwhelmed.

4. You are on the freeze/shutdown floor. Recall the recent memory of when you felt emotionally shut down or disconnected from others. As you hold this memory, engage your five senses in that specific environment and just notice:

   · What did you see? What were you touching? What sounds were present? Were there any smells or tastes?

   · How did your body respond to the situation in both small and big ways? Did you cross your arms, stop speaking, or become significantly tired?

- What's happening to your body now? What gets activated on this floor?

5. Take a few deep breaths and then head toward the elevator. Take it to the second floor, the fight-or-flight floor. As you step out of the elevator, remind yourself you can exit at any time if you feel too overwhelmed.

6. Recall the recent memory of when you felt an impulse to confront someone or get away. As you hold this memory, engage your five senses in that specific environment and just notice:

   - What did you see? What were you touching? What sounds were present? Were there any smells or tastes?

   - How did your body respond to the situation in both small and big ways? Did your body become constricted? Did your heart rate increase? Did you become confrontational or impulsively remove yourself from the situation?

   - What's happening to your body now? What gets activated on this floor?

7. Take a few deep breaths and then head toward the elevator. Take it to the top floor, the social engagement floor.

8. Recall the recent memory of when you felt safe and connected to others. As you hold this memory, engage your five senses in that specific environment and just notice.

   - What did you see? What were you touching? What sounds were present? Were there any smells or tastes?

   - How did your body respond to the situation in both small and big ways? Did your body become calmer? Were you more social? Did you connect to a person in a particular way? Was it through physical touch? Did the environment stimulate you in a positive way?

- What's happening to your body now? What gets activated on this floor?

9. You can either hang out on the social engagement floor a while longer or take the elevator down to the bottom floor, leave the building, and reorient yourself to the present moment.

Modification

If you have ever had a traumatic experience with elevators, you can visualize a staircase instead. Also, if noticing your body sensations feels too overwhelming right now, externalize this exercise by speculating how others may experience similar situations. In other words, instead of drawing from your own experiences, recall times when you witnessed a person (1) acting emotionally disconnected, (2) acting emotionally charged up, and (3) connecting well with others.

Journal Prompt

Describe the shifts you noticed in your body. If possible, name the body sensations that occurred on each "floor of the building." In what types of scenarios do you find yourself on the freeze/shutdown floor? Who can still reach you? Who do you shut out? What brings you back to a sense of connection with yourself and others?

The Empty Chair Technique

What You'll Need

- 15 to 20 minutes of uninterrupted time
- Journal and pen/pencil (or digital)
- Two facing chairs

The empty chair technique is one of the oldest and most well-researched interventions in psychotherapy that assists folks in expressing/releasing emotions, thoughts, and body sensations that were once repressed. Often used in psychodrama therapy, this technique was developed by German psychiatrist Fritz Perls, the founder of Gestalt therapy, a type of psychotherapy. The focus of the empty chair technique is on being in the present moment while exploring aspects of the self. This is a practice of honoring and expressing your feelings and gaining insight into how extensive your feelings are.

The empty chair, which you will sit across from, serves as a representation of a person (e.g., a parent, partner, friend, or enemy) or a part of yourself (e.g., a younger self or a part that frustrates you). This exercise gives you an opportunity to release unexpressed feelings, emotions, and body sensations and resolve internal conflicts or emotions around a relationship/experience with someone else or yourself.

During this exercise, you can get to know aspects of yourself better by focusing on yourself tapping into unspoken feelings and thoughts and openly expressing them. Folks often release feelings of anger, anxiety, and other bottled-up emotions and grieve for whatever might have been lost in the present. Essentially, this technique is about finally expressing feelings that once were pushed down.

Note There is no right or wrong way to do this technique. In fact, you don't even have to use a chair; you can sit on a pillow facing an empty pillow. Also, you can close your eyes if you'd like or even write what you want to say in your journal if you don't want to speak aloud. If you become overwhelmed during this exercise, stand up, stretch, and move around to discharge some of the emotion to reset yourself before continuing.

Instructions

1. Sit in your calm, quiet space on a chair with an empty chair across from you.

2. Notice the contact of the ground against your feet, the contact of your seat against the chair, and your arms and hands making contact with a surface. Practice noticing sensations, contact, pressure, and texture on/in your body.

3. Look at the chair across from you. Bring to mind a person you have an unresolved issue with or a part of yourself you are frustrated with. To start, choose a person or aspect of yourself that's around a 3 or 4 on a distress scale of 0 to 10, with 10 being the most distressing and 0 being not distressing at all.

4. Imagine this person or aspect is sitting across from you. Visualize them in detail. How do they look? What do they have on? Does anything about them stand out?

5. Think about the feelings you have toward this person or part of yourself. Take some time to feel the feelings in your body. Don't attempt to push them down; go toward them.

6. Openly express your feelings to whomever is in the empty chair, being as direct as you can and not curbing your speech. If you need to shout or use a tone you're not used to, go for it!

7. Release every thought and feeling of being connected to that person or part of you. Even if a thought feels small or irrelevant, release it. If you feel like moving parts of your body, do it. Try your best to get everything out.

8. Once you feel that you have fully expressed your thoughts and feelings, gently shake your body to release tension and settle down. Take a deep breath and ground yourself by engaging your five senses.

Journal Prompt

What did you notice about yourself as you expressed your feelings? What emotions or thoughts were easy to express? What emotions or thoughts were harder to express? What sensations did you feel in your body? Where in your body were you holding these feelings?

Exaggerating to Identify, Honor, Connect, and Express

What You'll Need

- 15 to 20 minutes of uninterrupted time
- Journal and pen/pencil (or digital)

Some people struggle with identifying and expressing their feelings. To help clients in this area, a therapist who specializes in Gestalt therapy may encourage a client to exaggerate a particular body movement, expression, or tone as they speak about a particular topic to help them become aware of the emotion that's attached to that action. Let's say a client is talking about their boss's heated email but isn't expressing to the therapist how they felt about it. The therapist notices that the client's right leg is bouncing slightly as they discuss the matter, and so the therapist encourages the client to exaggerate that body movement. Doing this gives the client insight into how that heated email brought up feelings in them that they then repressed and further helps the client recognize the connection between their emotions and body.

This exercise will help you identify, honor, connect to, and express your emotions, body sensations, and parts of yourself that you may often repress or dismiss. Exaggerating your body movement or tone of expression brings attention to feelings that you intellectualize and gives them momentum. Furthermore, it reminds you that no feeling is too big or bothersome and that you can give it room to take up as much space as it needs. Overall, it allows the body to expand and release, safely allowing the body to complete and discharge its energy.

Note This exercise focuses on releasing anger by exaggerating a body movement, but other things can be exaggerated as well, like tone of voice, facial expressions, etc. You may even want to snarl or growl. You can repeat and exaggerate anything that safely allows your body to discharge the energy. The repeated exaggeration does not have to be outwardly noticeable—for example, if you feel constriction in your body, you can further constrict that part of your body by tensing the area.

Instructions

1. Sit in your calm, quiet space. Prepare yourself with a recent memory of mild to moderate distress or frustration where you felt some level of anger; you may have either dismissed the anger or didn't have a safe enough space to express it completely.

2. Notice the contact of the ground against your feet, the contact of your seat against a chair, and your arms and hands making contact with a surface. Practice noticing sensations, contact, pressure, and texture on/in your body.

3. Close your eyes or gaze down, and bring the memory you identified to mind. Notice if any part of your body feels constricted, tight, jumpy, nervous, agitated, irritated, or numb.

4. Lean into the body sensation and slowly begin to exaggerate it by making it bigger. For example, if your hands are shaking slightly, start shaking them more rapidly, letting all the energy connected to them evaporate.

5. Continue to hold the memory in mind, and slowly tighten the body part for 5 seconds (e.g., make a tight fist), and then release it and take a deep breath.

6. Exaggerate the movement again to its fullness for 10 to 15 seconds, and then tighten that body part again for 5 seconds, releasing it as you breathe out.

7. Release any more residue connected to the anger by exaggerating the body part and then slowly letting the movement fall away.

8. When you are done, repeat step 2 to ground yourself.

Journal Prompt

Write about the recent memory you identified in detail, but this time, describe the exaggerated expression as part of the memory, fully feeling and describing the gap of that missed emotion. Reflect on how the memory feels different now that the feeling has been fully expressed.

A Gradual Invitation to Sadness and Disappointment

What You'll Need

- 15 to 30 minutes of uninterrupted time
- Journal and pen/pencil (or digital)

Many of us were raised in homes where particular emotions were not accepted. One emotion that's often shunned is sadness, along with its close partner, disappointment. If sadness and disappointment were discouraged or dismissed during your childhood, a part of you will now attempt to avoid or repress those emotions. When they do arise, the ability to manage them is lacking. You need to have a relationship with an emotion and be able to know it, recognize it, and understand it before you can manage it. This means first learning to sit with it.

In this exercise, you will gradually invite in disappointment and sadness and learn to feel these emotions and then release them. When you openly invite a feeling in rather than trying to avoid it, any anxiety or fear connected to feeling that emotion will dissipate. On the other hand, if you continue to avoid feeling these emotions, it reinforces the fear or anxiety of experiencing them. You'll also get to know the avoiding/protector part of yourself that wants you to push these emotions away and become aware of its impulse to either fight, flee, or freeze when confronted by these emotions. This insight can help you fully process and release the emotion more readily in the future.

Some version of this exercise is essentially used in every kind of therapy. For example, a therapist may simply let you sit with an emotion that arises, while another may verbally instruct you to sit with it. Therapists know that expanding your ability to hold your emotions will expand your windows of tolerance (see page 62) and consequently teach you how to process the emotions outside your practice.

Note This exercise may uncover some type of blockage; our survival instinct wants to avoid pain and anything that reminds us of it, erroneously thinking that pain will lead to death. Therefore, an essential part of this exercise includes communicating to yourself that you are safe, despite the discomfort you may feel. Safety is the main ingredient you need to have in place when submitting yourself to processing difficult memories and emotions. Remind yourself that this is a gradual process and that developing a relationship with an emotion takes time.

Instructions

1. Sit in your calm, quiet space. Prepare yourself with two recent memories of disappointment. The first should be a 2 or 3 on a distress scale of 0 to 10 and the other a higher level, perhaps a 5 or 6, with 10 being the most distressing and 0 being not distressing at all.

2. Notice the contact of the ground against your feet, the contact of your seat against a chair, and your arms and hands making contact with a surface. Practice noticing sensations, contact, pressure, and texture on/in your body.

3. Close your eyes or gaze down and slowly bring to mind the first memory with lower-intensity disappointment. Notice the feeling of disappointment and let sadness naturally show up; grief may show up as well. Let them take up space.

4. Give yourself permission to feel these emotions. You may feel them as an external body sensation or an internal feeling. Allow them to be there for 15 to 30 seconds. Notice the intensity of the feelings. There's no need to respond to the feelings; just let them be.

5. Now, mentally, take a step back and observe the feelings. Take a deep breath.

6. Rock, sway, or touch the area that was activated, and remind your body that it is safe to be here. Take another deep breath.

7. Slowly bring to mind the second memory with the higher level of disappointment, and repeat steps 4 to 6.

8. To close, do the 5-4-3-2-1 Grounding Technique on page 66.

Journal Prompt

Describe the two memories you worked with in this exercise. When you felt the disappointment and sadness, did part of you shift into protective mode? Did you have an urge or impulse to fight against them or get away from them (fight or flight)? Did you want to shut down (freeze)? Reflect on this protective part of you. Describe how it felt to sit with these feelings and observe them.

Updating Your Memory Files

What You'll Need

- 15 to 20 minutes of uninterrupted time
- Journal and pen/pencil (or digital)

One of the most healing experiences in therapy is when a client is processing a moment in life when they were voiceless, and during the session, they verbalize the thoughts and feelings they were unable to express at the time. This technique isn't limited to voiceless moments, though—physical expressions and feelings may also be repressed.

Imagine your memories are stored in your mind, like an office filled with filing cabinets categorized by age. When you are processing a memory in trauma healing work or just in general, you go into that office and choose a file, review it, and then insert new information from your adult self. This adult self speaks up for your needs, perhaps tells you it wasn't your fault, or completes something you weren't able to do or verbalize at the time. After inserting this new information into the file, you place it back in the filing cabinet and exit the office.

A large part of healing in attachment-based therapy and psycho-dynamic therapy is when a "corrective" emotional experience occurs. This is when a client pulls out one of those memory files, reflects on or reenacts a memory of a time when they lacked emotional support, and the therapist provides what they needed in the present moment, essentially correcting the inner child's perception of that experience. Ongoing moments of corrective emotional experiences begin to heal the wounds connected to those experiences.

In this exercise, you will provide your inner child with the support you lacked in situations where you felt voiceless, immobile, unheard, unseen, etc. You will learn to complete the uncompleted moments of your childhood, essentially updating, correcting, or completing the files you've stored away.

Note With this exercise, you are beginning the process of tending to your inner child and meeting their unmet needs. You won't be embodying your younger self; rather, you will be responding to your younger self as your adult self. If you feel hesitation around exploring a childhood memory right now, revisit a more recent memory of a time you had "unfinished business." Come back to this exercise when you feel ready to explore a childhood memory.

Instructions

1. Sit in your calm, quiet space. Prepare yourself with a non-traumatic childhood memory of a time when your voice or expression was repressed. Start with something you'd rate a 3 on a distress scale of 0 to 10, with 10 being the most distressing and 0 being not distressing at all.

2. Notice the contact of the ground against your feet, the contact of your seat against a chair, and your arms and hands making contact with a surface. Practice noticing sensations, contact, pressure, and texture on/in your body.

3. Close your eyes or gaze down, and bring to mind the memory you identified.

4. Once you have the memory in mind, imagine that you are in an office filled with filing cabinets categorized by age. Pull out the file for the memory you want to tend to and open it.

5. Imagine now that you are looking at your younger self. Notice the feelings that come up for you. Remind your body that it is present and safe.

6. Take a deep breath, and recall each of the five senses connected to that memory. What did you see, hear, touch, smell, and/or taste?

7. What did your younger self need to say or do? Did they need to hear something? Whatever it is, slowly say or do whatever the younger you couldn't say or do. Tell them what they needed to hear. Repeat the words or actions multiple times until you feel complete.

8. Close the file, put it back in the cabinet, and exit the office. Take a deep breath.

9. Think about any recent memories where you had a similar experience. Say aloud what you needed to say, or perform an action. Take another deep breath.

10. To close, perform the 5-4-3-2-1 Grounding Technique on page 66.

Journal Prompt

Reflect on any emotions and responses that came up for you when you visualized your younger self. Describe the "memory file" you worked with. How did you update it before refiling it? Describe similar situations in your adult life where you felt as your younger self did. List ways you can complete some uncompleted moments.

Chapter 7

Reconnecting to Your Body

The body deserves a dedicated space to feel, release, and rest. Redeveloping our relationship with our bodies reframes how we interact and respond to our childhood trauma. We now know that psychological pain manifesting as physical symptoms (i.e., the somatization of trauma) is something that can happen to anyone who has experienced trauma. The only difference is how folks uniquely hold and metabolize trauma in their bodies.

A key indicator of healing trauma is when someone becomes aware of how their body holds and expresses their history; this enables them to identify techniques that will release and settle their body, thereby reducing the intensity of their body's reactions when triggers show up. That's what the exercises in this chapter aim to help you do.

Body Scan

What You'll Need

- 15 to 30 minutes of uninterrupted time
- Journal and pen/pencil (or digital)

The body scan is deeply connected to Buddhist practice and has been around for centuries. In 1979, Jon Kabat-Zinn brought this practice to the Western world with his development of mindfulness-based stress reduction (MBSR), an evidence-based therapy that helps reduce symptoms of stress, anxiety, depression, and physical pain. The body scan is the first mindfulness exercise taught in MBSR, and it is the basis of gaining awareness and developing a relationship with our bodies.

In completing the body scan, you will take an inventory of your mind and body in a gentle manner. You will learn to give time, care, and attention to your whole body by systematically scanning different body parts—from the top of the head to the soles of the feet.

This exercise provides a wealth of physical and emotional benefits, including grounding you and helping you release areas of tension in different parts of your body. However, what particularly stands out is the development and deepening of the relationship with the body. You will learn to continuously go to your body in a gentle, nonjudgmental manner, sending a message to your psyche that you are worthy enough to engage with. Over time, you may find that the practice transforms from an exercise of relaxation to a practice of self-compassion and self-love

Note This exercise can feel intimidating at first because you may want to avoid certain parts of your body. That's OK. If it feels too intense to give an area attention, minimize the time spent on that area or skip it. If you tend to struggle with your attention span, you may feel this isn't for you, but if you work through it, you may find that the body scan actually helps improve your attention span. In any event, it's normal to become distracted during this exercise; just notice the distraction without interacting with it and shift your attention back to your body.

Instructions

1. Sit or lie in your calm, quiet space (play soothing music, if desired). Take a deep breath, and close your eyes or gaze down.

2. Set an intention to scan your body without judgment. Just observe and acknowledge your body sensations and your overall self.

3. Notice the top of your head, and then slowly observe your mind and thoughts without responding to them.

4. Take a deep breath and continue scanning your body, observing any sensations in those areas and noting without judgment if the muscles are loose, constricted, or neutral. Take a deep breath between each group and as needed. Follow this sequence:

   - Face, forehead, eyes, nose, and cheeks

   - Neck and shoulder area

   - Right arm and hand along with each finger and fingertip

   - Left arm and hand along with each finger and fingertip

   - Chest

   - Stomach

   - Back and bottom

- Thighs, knees, calves, and ankles

- The tops of the feet and the soles of the feet along with each toe

5. Take a final deep breath to complete the scan.

Journal Prompt

How was your experience with the body scan? Did any parts of your body stand out to you as being "good" or "bad"? Part by part, describe the body sensations connected to each. Reflect on areas of the body that felt easy to give attention to.

Tension Release and Self-Soothing

What You'll Need

- 15 to 30 minutes of uninterrupted time
- Journal and pen/pencil (or digital)

This is a four-part exercise that involves tension release and self-soothing practices that assist in releasing trauma that's stuck in the body. Patterns of anxiety, stress, and trauma can build up deep in our muscles, leading to health issues and emotional disturbances. Finding ways to release this buildup is essential to healing trauma. Activities like vibrating, shaking, or swaying can bail out the tension in the muscles, resulting in a lighter, more flexible, and more balanced body.

But how does this buildup occur in the first place? As you may recall, when we are faced with a threat, our bodies go into either fight-or-flight mode or freeze mode. When there's a power dynamic involved in a threat, a child is unlikely to be able to fight or flee successfully; therefore, the body turns to the freeze response. In this moment of freeze, muscle tension gets locked in the body. If it is not released soon after the stressful event, the body holds on to this traumatic memory.

There are many cultural and spiritual practices for releasing negative buildup in the body. Some examples include shaking, humming, and screaming. Many animals naturally engage in the process of "shaking off" tension. In fact, they literally shake their bodies after a stressful event; this is known as the tremor mechanism.

Note Tension-releasing and self-soothing exercises can be culturally specific. While we suggest trying each of the following four exercises to identify which feels most suitable to you, we also encourage you to research ways your ancestors traditionally released whatever they were holding in their bodies. Many indigenous cultures used dancing, chanting, or unique body movements, for example.

Instructions

Jaw Opening/Tongue Out (Purge Technique)

1. Sit in your calm, quiet space with your back supported, and close your eyes or gaze down. Notice the muscles in your face, and then place your attention on your jaw. Perform all the movements in steps 2 to 4 slowly.

2. Clench your jaw for 5 seconds, and then release it. Feel your face relaxing, and let your jaw rest for 5 seconds. Now open your jaw for 5 seconds. Notice the expansion, and then let it relax and rest for 10 seconds.

3. Move your jaw to the right, and then let it relax for 5 seconds. Move your jaw to the left, and then let it relax for 5 seconds. Make a circle with your jaw, and then let it relax for 10 seconds.

4. Stick out your tongue, stretching your jaw and face simultaneously to release whatever energy is stuck, for 5 seconds.

5. Take a deep breath, and then repeat the process if you'd like.

Humming with Rocking/Swaying

1. Sit in your calm, quiet space, and take a deep breath. Think about a song or rhythm that's easy for you to hum.

2. Begin to hum, noticing the vibrations in your throat, neck area, chest, and head.

3. Observe your body sensations as you continue to hum.

4. Slowly rock from side to side, gently swaying with the rhythm of the hum. Don't get caught up in matching the rhythm perfectly; just let your body move from side to side.

5. Continue rocking and humming for as long as you'd like.

Sighing and Vocalizing Tones

1. Sit in your calm, quiet space, and place your right hand on your stomach.

2. Inhale for 4 seconds, and hold your breath for 5 seconds.

3. Slowly release your breath for 8 to 10 seconds, making an *oooo*, *ahh*, or *vooo* sound.

4. Repeat the process three times.

Joints Movement and Body Melting

1. Stand in your calm, quiet space, and perform all the following movements slowly.

2. Rotate your neck three times.

3. Shift your attention to your arms, bend at the elbow, and rotate your arms three times.

4. Bring your focus to your wrists and rotate three times.

5. Shift your attention to your fingers, clenching and releasing three times.

6. Bring your attention to your hips and rotate three times.

7. Bring your attention all the way down to your ankles. Bend one knee, then the other, to rotate each ankle three times.

8. Take a deep breath and lie on your back with your knees slightly bent and your feet flat on the floor. Allow your arms to rest at your sides.

9. Slow your breathing and imagine that your body is melting into the floor.

10. If you notice any tension or anxiety in parts of your body, bring your attention to that area and imagine the tension melting into the floor.

Journal Prompt

Which of these exercises did you feel most comfortable doing? Why? Which of these exercises felt more difficult to complete? Why? What other tension-releasing exercises and self-soothing exercises might you want to try? Are any particular to your culture?

Bilateral Stimulation

What You'll Need

- 15 to 20 minutes of uninterrupted time
- Journal and pen/pencil (or digital)

Bilateral stimulation heightens communication between the brain's left and right hemispheres, activating memories, improving balance, enhancing flow, etc. Some examples of bilateral stimulation include tapping your knees or shoulders while alternating sides (left knee/shoulder and then right knee/shoulder), moving your eyes from left to right, swaying your hips from side to side, and focusing on sounds in your left ear and then your right ear. It is often associated with eye movement desensitization and reprocessing (EMDR) therapy because it is the primary skill used in EMDR when treating trauma. In this exercise, however, bilateral stimulation is being used as a stand-alone tool outside of EMDR for the purpose of settling and relaxing your body, *not* for reprocessing trauma. Here, you will be performing a "butterfly hug" and tapping your upper arms, alternating between the right and left sides.

The concept of bilateral stimulation has been around much longer than EMDR. Like many of the exercises in this book, it has been used in different cultures, including Sostenes's culture. Growing up in Brazil, Sostenes learned about the concept of "ginga" (pronounced *jinga*) in capoeira, a Brazilian martial art. This Portuguese word means "to swing." In capoeira, this refers to the ongoing side-to-side sway of the body, which includes footwork and is the basis of all capoeira movements.

There's a great deal of research that backs the benefits of bilateral stimulation, which includes a reduction of anxiety, stress, somatic (physical) symptoms, depression, worrisome thoughts, and trauma-related symptoms. When bilateral stimulation is performed while focusing on a positive event or pleasant visualization, there is an increase in creativity, happiness, and self-esteem, and parts of the unconscious become unlocked. Dr. Laurel Parnell has a great book called *Tapping In,* in which she discusses in depth how bilateral stimulation through physically tapping on the body can help us access, activate, and strengthen positive qualities such as calm, safety, and courage.

Note Bilateral stimulation is commonly performed through visual, auditory, tactile, or back-and-forth body movements. Once you have done this exercise, feel free to explore different kinds of bilateral stimulation to see what's most helpful to you.

Instructions

1. Sit in your calm, quiet space with your back supported, and close your eyes or gaze down. Take two deep breaths.

2. Imagine a real or imaginary place that you associate with calm or peace. If you'd like, you can use the place you identified in the Safe Place exercise on page 51.

3. As you imagine this place, focus on your five senses: What can you see, touch, smell, hear, and taste? Notice the feelings and sensations in your body as you hold the image in mind.

4. Cross your arms over your chest as if you are giving yourself a hug. Rest your right hand on the upper part of your left arm, and rest your left hand on the upper part of your right arm, as shown in the diagram.

5. Begin to tap your upper arms, not too slow and not too fast, alternating between your left arm and your right arm. As you tap, focus on positive body sensations or thoughts that may arise. Continue this back-and-forth tapping rhythmically for at least 45 seconds.

6. When finished, take a deep breath and orient yourself to your surroundings.

Journal Prompt

Did any interesting images, memories, or thoughts come up for you while tapping? What body sensations surfaced during this exercise? Did you focus on parts of your body while tapping? What other types of bilateral stimulation would you like to try, and which do you think would be most comfortable?

Befriending Your Body

What You'll Need

- 20 to 30 minutes of uninterrupted time
- Journal and pen/pencil (or digital)

There's a quote by poet and author Nayyirah Waheed we'd like to share with you since it so beautifully states the intention of this exercise: "And I said to my body, softly, 'I want to be your friend.' It took a long breath and replied, 'I have been waiting my whole life for this.'"

Our bodies are always looking for ways to heal and mend. Since you are working through this book and these exercises, you likely survived chronic and/or acute trauma and have experienced various forms of dissociation, detachment, and distance from yourself or your body. This is a protective mechanism that prevents us from *emotionally* and *mentally* holding the trauma. However, it does not prevent your *body* from holding on to it. In his book *The Body Keeps the Score: Brain, Mind, and Body in the Healing of Trauma,* Bessel van der Kolk talks about the importance of familiarizing oneself with the sensations in the body and then befriending those sensations to be able to recover from trauma.

Many times, when we've had traumatic experiences, we learn to respond to fear, sadness, terror, and/or even happiness with a dismissive, reactive, or hateful response. This response gets internalized, and we develop a hateful relationship toward ourselves and our body. However, when we can hold and befriend our body as well as its protective mechanisms and sensations, we develop more self-compassion for ourselves overall, which supports our entire nervous system to slowly shift into a more harmonious internal state.

In this exercise, you'll learn to befriend your body. As you move through this exercise, it's important *not* to place high expectations on yourself or how this is "supposed to go." Remain openhearted and use the curiosity you've been cultivating. Noticing and befriending your body from afar is valuable, even if you can only imagine an inkling of friendship right now. Give yourself permission to start wherever you are.

Note If you are presently in conflict with your body, and it seems easier to use this current experience in step 1, that's fine. However, a great place to begin befriending your body is with a memory or time when you felt at war with yourself or as if your body was "against you."

Instructions

1. Sit in your calm, quiet space with your journal handy, and bring to mind a memory or situation that you would rate a 2 or 3 on a distress scale of 0 to 10 in which you felt your body was the "enemy," with 10 being the most distressing and 0 being not distressing at all. (You can work with higher ratings later.)

2. Try to create a sense of distance and space from the sensations and memory of this experience as you notice, observe, and journal whatever is coming up for you. If you sense a constriction or tension in your body, try to put a name to this.

3. Explore the following questions in your journal—just notice what's coming up as you ask these questions, acknowledge what you are noticing, and write it down:

   - What was some of the messaging that your body received during this time?

   - What was it being blamed for?

   - When did it start to carry the message of being the enemy?

   - What were some of the blocks that prevented you from befriending your body?

4. Remind yourself that you're just exploring; there is no shame or criticism in having these blocks. Honor them and recognize their value for that time of your life. If the blocks are still present today, it is likely they are serving some purpose, but the goal here is to just explore what these blocks are.

5. If you begin to feel too overwhelmed or detached from your body, pause, focus on your breath, and do the 5-4-3-2-1 Grounding Technique on page 66 before moving on.

6. Name some of the external forces that prevented or blocked you from connecting to your body. Acknowledge the protective armor your body has used to protect you, and offer it your gratitude. Recall and acknowledge those times when your body did not receive the validation and support it needed to recover and heal.

7. Take a deep breath. Acknowledge where you are with your efforts to repair your relationship with your body.

Journal Prompt

Describe your experience doing this exercise. Which parts did you struggle with? Which did you find particularly moving or meaningful?

Showing Your Body Gentleness

What You'll Need

- 20 to 40 minutes of uninterrupted time
- Journal and pen/pencil (or digital)
- Scented or unscented body oil or lotion
- Mood-setting items such as cushions, blankets, candles, or soft music

This exercise helps you begin to create a positive association between your body and mind to assist you in reframing and healing from trauma. When we are gentle to our bodies, our natural self-healing wisdom, which may have been lying dormant, is reawakened. A gentle practice opens the door for unwavering trust to develop between mind and body. It increases positive communication in which both the body and the mind can rely on the other to respond to anything "bad" or "negative" with gentleness. This stimulates a creative, subtle, interesting part of ourselves that often goes overlooked in our busy lives.

Unfortunately, the world often communicates that our bodies are not enough, often in violent or displeasing ways. To counteract this messaging, we need to do the opposite—that is, be gentle with and kind to the body. This isn't easy, however; it takes consistent practice. Often, the inner critic will show up and try to start a conflict with the body, especially if it notices a sensation of discomfort. This is an avoidant/survival part that only feeds the anxiety connected to the sensation. Gentleness, softness, and compassion toward the body can reduce the inner critic's voice, giving you the opportunity to care for the body part that deserves your attention. This initiates a feeling of aliveness in the body and helps you heal from dissociation, detachment, and disconnection from self and others.

Note It's completely up to you to set up your space in any way that feels comfortable and relaxing. The same is true for the body-care products you use. Tailor this exercise to your preferences and what you have readily available.

Instructions

1. Go to your calm, quiet space and set the mood for a relaxing experience.

2. Apply a drop of body oil or lotion to your feet. Move your hands in small circular motions. Notice how it feels to receive a massage from yourself.

3. Alternate between harder and lighter pressure, circular motions, strokes, and pressing/releasing. Pay attention to what pressure and motion you prefer.

4. Work your way up your legs, starting with one leg and moving to the other leg, spending at least a minute on each leg.

5. As you are engaging in this massage, repeat an affirmation such as "You are so deserving of this love, this touch, and this connection" or "You are beautiful just the way you are."

6. Continue to massage your body wherever your hands lead you. If there are any parts of your body to which you have a strong aversion, notice it, tell this part of you that it's welcome, and then move on to the next body part.

7. Continue offering touch, while noticing texture and smell as well as how your body responds to this activity. If any urges or impulses emerge to hurt or harm yourself, notice that and allow yourself to discharge the energy by doing one of the Tension Release and Self-Soothing exercises on pages 127–130.

8. End this time with yourself by offering gratitude to your body. Stretch, yawn, and release.

Modification

If you are physically unable to do any part of this exercise, adjust or modify it to fit your needs. If you prefer to begin in a place other than your feet, feel free to change up the order of body parts.

Journal Prompt

Did you have any hesitation engaging with this exercise? How was the experience for you to touch and massage yourself using a positive affirmation? Was there any particular part of this exercise that seemed particularly noteworthy?

Part Four

Strengthening Your Core Self

Chapter 8

Reparenting and Parts Work

Have you ever felt multiple desires and opinions of yourself existing at the same time? Perhaps a part of you wants to take on a new job and tackle the challenges presented, but another part of you feels comfortable and at ease and does not want to change things up. These are parts of you that hold feelings, beliefs, memories, and roles within your internal system. The exercises in this chapter will help you learn to explore and have compassion for these different parts and to cultivate a stronger anchor in yourself to guide wounded and younger parts of you into a harmonious system.

This type of exploration and practice is an essential part of healing trauma work. This is because trauma fragments our memories, beliefs, and emotions, which can be lost, go unnoticed, and/or become disconnected from our awareness. As we begin trauma healing, we seek integration, resolution, and healing for our younger parts so we may feel more at ease, more compassionate, and more whole as a person.

Gathering around the Campfire

What You'll Need

- 20 to 30 minutes of uninterrupted time
- Figurines to represent different aspects of your younger self (optional)
- Drawing paper and pen/pencil (optional)
- Journal and pen/pencil (or digital)

As you learned in chapter 5, the Internal Family Systems Model (IFS) theorizes that we each have a core self as well as various parts or sub-parts of ourselves that form during childhood, which we may or may not be conscious of and which may sometimes be in conflict. Building on your work in the Befriending Your Many Parts exercise on page 91, you'll now practice creating an "internal listening" space where you can practice listening, being in connection with, and holding space for multiple parts of yourself, specifically younger versions of yourself at various stages of development.

Oftentimes, your inner child (those younger versions of you) may have gone unnoticed, unattended to, or even shamed or ridiculed for normal emotions and human needs. Meeting and spending time with your younger parts gives them an opportunity to be acknowledged and heard, providing valuable information and context, and may perhaps bring up unexpressed, unidentified, and repressed feelings.

Note In chapter 3, you identified your "internal nurturing figure" (see page 54). It's valuable to bring in this figure now to serve as your compass and regulator to support your work as you learn to hold space and compassion for your inner child. Moreover, in Befriending Your Many Parts on page 91, you began identifying your various parts in step 2 before working specifically with just one. Now, you can work with some of the others.

Instructions

1. Go to your calm, quiet space with any supplies you may be using.

2. Either on paper, with your figurines, or in your imagination, "build" a campfire and place enough chairs around the fire to accommodate all the versions of yourself you are inviting to join you, as well as your internal nurturing figure.

3. Bring in your grounded, compassionate, calm adult self to hold space for the younger parts of you. Take a seat.

4. Now, begin to invite in different parts of yourself. Acknowledge your parts as they show up and allow them to come and go at their own pace. Be sure to include the "managerial" part of you (which in IFS terminology is the part or parts of you that tend to want to control, manage, and keep everything functioning, and usually want to keep emotional parts at bay). Also be sure to include the "firefighter"—in IFS, this is the part that stays braced for any potential danger and is ready to swoop in to avoid the experience of overwhelming emotions or pain at any cost.

5. Notice the age of each part as it enters the scene. When was the first time you remember feeling or noticing that part of you?

6. You may place these parts wherever you would like around the campfire and wherever these parts feel at ease or comfortable. If one part of you would like to hang back away from the fire, allow them to do so; your parts may show up in whatever way they feel safe. If any of your parts do not feel comfortable showing up, give space and permission for this, too.

7. If you feel you have enough capacity to also hold space for any particular part or parts, write down or explore anything that comes to mind and that you may be aware of with regard to that part of you.

8. Finally, thank each part of you for coming to the fire in whatever capacity they were able to, and allow them to leave whenever they need to.

9. Close out the exercise by orienting yourself to your surroundings. Take in the colors, textures, and temperature of the room. Inhale for a count of four and exhale for six. Move and shake your body, continuing to release with a forceful exhale and Jaw Opening/Tongue Out response (see page 128).

Journal Prompt

How was this exercise? Did you feel overwhelmed at any point? What came up for you as your different parts entered the campfire space? How did you find your way back to your grounded self? Is there anything that struck you as particularly significant?

Meeting Your Inner Child at Milestone Ages

What You'll Need

- 15 to 30 minutes of uninterrupted time
- Journal and pen/pencil (or digital)

Our mind tends to identify milestone ages of our younger self that we feel best encapsulate or categorize a childhood experience. Maybe it's a five-year-old holding a puppy with silky ears or a six-year-old pulling the red wagon or a seven-year-old climbing a tree. You can use whatever represents an aspect of your younger self (e.g., an image, clothing article, toy) to connect with and get to know yourself better.

As you've learned, whatever happens during our childhood gets etched into our psyche and into our body tissues and nervous system. The body and mind continue to tell these stories in various ways. When faced with a trigger, our mind and body will jump back to the age when the trauma was most severe, and it will believe we are that child again, whether five or fifteen years old. This is why we may throw a childlike tantrum or cling to a partner or cut everyone out of our life when we really want people to lean on and trust. This is our younger self, the inner child, who is present and active and is asking for what was never given to them during those younger years.

With this exercise, you will select three milestones from your childhood of different developmental years to spend more time getting to know this younger child/adolescent part of yourself better. You'll have the opportunity to acknowledge what wasn't available, what was so painful about that time, and the hard things you didn't deserve to experience, but also the good sorts of things you *do* deserve to have and experience now—safety, love, freedom, autonomy, and connection, to name a few.

Although part of you may feel resistant to bringing up painful memories from those ages, your inner child has had these experiences and is intruding on your life in various ways—you may just be trying to ignore or suppress it. Forming a relationship and connecting to the younger you can change the way this part of you asks for attention in the future.

Note Allow the experience to emerge naturally. Don't "force" or try to "conjure up" anything. If your younger self is distant and estranged from you and is not open to connecting, that's OK. Acknowledge and start where your younger self is. Your inner child might be like a stray, fearful puppy; you may have to continually show up from a distance and provide for its needs to build trust. It could take weeks or months until it allows you close enough to touch it. Your inner child may need to maintain their distance and mistrust for now—and that's OK.

Instructions

1. Sit in your calm, quiet space with your art supplies handy. Bring to mind yourself at three different ages that you'd like to explore and get to know better.

2. Write each age on a separate page of your journal. This will serve as a place for you to explore that version of yourself. Choose one age to begin with. Place that child in the safe place you visualized in the exercise on page 51.

3. Notice what the child is wearing, how they are acting or responding, and what emotions are showing up on their face. Bring in curiosity and observation. What do you notice when you bring up this image of your inner child?

4. Does your inner child notice your presence? If it feels right, slowly interact with this version of yourself. Do not force anything to happen. Simply observe with curiosity. Allow a scene to play out if you

feel calm and regulated. However, if you notice strong impulses to stop, rescue, or "fix" the child, use one of your resources such as grounding (see page 66) or breathwork (see page 48).

5. If you made contact with your younger self, take a moment to say goodbye, and let them know you'll be back to check in later (be sure to do so another time). Take any notes in your journal about your time with that part of you.

6. Repeat these steps for the other ages or come back to them at a later time.

7. When you are done, reorient yourself to your surroundings and do something completely different such as having something to eat or drink, going for a walk, engaging in physical exercise, or taking a nap.

Journal Prompt

How was the exercise for you? What did you like or dislike about it? Did any part of you struggle with this exercise? Send a positive affirmation to any part of you that was unable to settle or remain with your younger self. This isn't unusual, and it is completely OK. Acknowledge your efforts, and give yourself time.

Drawing or Painting Your Inner Child

What You'll Need

- 15 to 30 minutes of uninterrupted time
- Art supplies preferred by your younger self such as paint, crayons, or colored pencils
- Drawing paper
- Journal and pen/pencil (or digital)

In his book *Playing and Reality,* pediatrician and psychoanalyst Donald Woods Winnicott writes, "It is only in being creative that the individual discovers the self." This exercise, which is meant to be playful, fun, and relaxed, helps you access your creativity and intuition by helping you connect to your younger self.

Because art and creativity allow for aspects of yourself to emerge without verbal processing, intellectualization, or analysis, you can use imagery, poetry, shapes, and colors to make sense of an experience. This is the language of children who are engaging in the world and lack the ability to analyze their experience and environment. When you set aside your adult expectations and refrain from trying to analyze what you produce through playful outlets, such as any art that emerges, you allow yourself to be discovered in new and creative ways.

Note Allow anything to come through at its own pace. Refrain from analyzing your drawing. Practice observing and noticing without offering any feedback or criticism. If you would like to comment, simply state an observation—e.g., "I see that you chose the red and yellow here" or "I can see you drawing with long strokes, wow."

1. Sit in your calm, quiet space with your art supplies handy, and take a minute to relax yourself with a couple deep breaths.

2. Using your nondominant hand, begin drawing. Give your younger self full rein and allow whatever emerges to come through. Don't force your younger self to do anything they are not comfortable with. If they are resistant about making art, acknowledge that as valuable and give them time, respecting their no.

3. Keep your heart open. Your inner child may be frightened, sad, scared, or bubbly. Practice accepting *all* of this part of you just as they are. Whatever they may draw or create for you is *valuable*.

4. Continue to spend time with your younger self, either by making art or engaging in a playful game together on the paper, such as tic-tac-toe.

5. Close out the time by thanking your inner child for showing up in whatever form or fashion they were comfortable with and acknowledge the time you had together.

Journal Prompt

What do you wish was noticed about your younger self? What were you proud of? What were you good at? What did this part of you crave?

Being Present with Your Inner Child

What You'll Need
- 15 to 30 minutes of uninterrupted time
- Journal and pen/pencil (or digital)

Childhood is when we learn to process and make sense of our emotions and experiences, but the truth of the matter is that many people experience emotionally unattuned, unavailable, or immature parents/caregivers, which can negatively impact our development. Consistently not having our emotional needs met can be a deeply damaging experience. This can show up as "attachment panic"—the internal panic of not being able to access/reach our caregiver—or the sense of losing our connection to ourselves, our power, or our self-agency.

The process of reparenting can be done in two different ways. There's the reparenting process when the therapist serves as a stand-in attachment figure for the client and provides reassurance, and there's the reparenting process in which you recall memories of your younger self and offer yourself a corrective emotional experience. As the adult, you stand in as the comforting, nurturing attachment figure. In this exercise, you'll practice noticing your younger self who may be carrying around wounds, feeling unnoticed, invalidated, or disbelieved, or perhaps feeling judged or rejected.

Note If at any point during this exercise you notice that you are feeling flooded or overwhelmed to the point where you start to zone out, shut down, or experience other intense emotions, refocus on nurturing and settling yourself and take a break from the exercise. You can come back to it whenever you are ready.

Instructions

1. Sit in your calm, quiet space with your journal handy.

2. Do the 5-4-3-2-1 Grounding Technique on page 66 to orient yourself to your surroundings.

3. Take a deep breath and open your journal. Respond to these prompts:

   - What did you long for your caregiver to notice or affirm about you?

   - Was there a certain way you wished they were able to show up for you?

   - What was painful about how they did or did not respond to you?

4. Now, explore a specific childhood wound that you are familiar with (e.g., unnoticed, invalidated, disbelieved, villainized, misunderstood, unheard, unaccepted, or voiceless). Notice your younger self when that wound initially occurred. What is your younger self wearing? What is the look on their face?

5. Bring in your "internal nurturing figure" (see page 54). How do you notice them (e.g., is there warmth, comfort, a sensation of being held, or of feeling safe)? Embrace this sense as you move forward.

6. Let yourself sense into the nurturing presence to be with your younger self. Just imagining the "presence with" is enough. There's never a need to make anything happen or to force an interaction. Allow your body to pause and take this in for a few minutes.

7. To close, bring your attention outside yourself and into your environment. Look around yourself and sense your feet on the ground. Breathe deeply and then exhale and shake.

Journal Prompt

Describe your experience with this exercise. How did it feel to be present with your younger self? How did your younger self feel in the presence of your internal nurturing figure?

Shadow Work

- 20 to 35 minutes of uninterrupted time
- Journal and pen/pencil (or digital)

What exactly is shadow work and why would anyone want to get to know their shadow parts? Carl Jung describes the shadow as the repressed desires of our unconscious mind—parts of our self that we've repressed and neglected for fear they won't be accepted or, even worse, will be judged as evil or bad by others. Jungian teacher and analyst James Hollis describes this as the parts of his personality he'd find troubling and would be the opposite of what he values and intends. So, yes, it seems counterintuitive to engage with the parts of us that are upsetting, unsettling, troubling, and confusing; however, when we ignore and outcast the shadow parts of ourselves, they end up intruding in our lives and becoming destructive. They can only be repressed for so long before they find a way to get our attention.

Imagine hearing an unsettling noise in the basement. Would you go downstairs to find the source? Are you terrified of what might be lurking there? Do you go down to tend to it? Do you block it out as a nuisance, thinking it's unlikely that anything important is going on down there? Perhaps you think there's nothing of value in the basement so why bother going down at all? This exercise invites you to look for the source of the noise. Here's your opportunity to start exploring the shadow parts of yourself that you might rather push out of your awareness or even disown when they pop up.

Note If your trauma is linked to your religious experience (i.e., religious trauma) or events that involved serious shame and judgment around normal human behaviors, then this shadow work exercise may be particularly triggering for you. We recommend working with a therapist who is trained in religious trauma to support you in the shadow parts of yourself that have been blocked or exiled from your awareness.

Instructions

1. Sit in your calm, quiet space with your journal handy. Take a deep breath and bring to mind a person who triggers you. In your journal, reflect on the following:

   - What about this person bothers you?

   - What is the story you tell yourself about them?

   - What does your reaction to this person tell you about yourself?

   - Do you share some traits with this person?

   - What part in you gets activated by this person?

   - How do you feel about this part?

2. Can you recognize one of your shadow parts in your reflections? Describe it if you can. As you explore this shadow part, do you feel an impulse to shut it down? Disown it? Invalidate it? If so, practice validating the purpose of this:

   - Did others want you to hide your weakness or vulnerabilities?

   - Did others only praise you when you were obedient and submissive?

   - Did you only get attention when you rebelled?

   - What else might have factored in?

3. If you are feeling grounded and safe, continue with these optional deepening steps; otherwise, skip to step 4:

- What parts of your maternal or paternal figure do you despise and/or have anger or distrust toward? (This can be valuable information about your relationship toward yourself and your wounds.)

- What parts of your maternal or paternal figure do you admire? Just hang out in curiosity, observing, noticing, and welcoming in any information without making meaning of whatever comes up.

4. Close out the exercise by orienting yourself to your surroundings. Take in the colors, textures, and temperature of the room. Inhale for a count of four and exhale for six. Move and shake your body.

Journal Prompt

How does it feel to explore your shadow parts? Did you do the optional step? Why or why not? How can you practice holding space for your shadow parts more often?

Chapter 9
Reclaiming Agency and Wholeness

A power dynamic often takes place in childhood trauma, leaving survivors feeling powerless, voiceless, and subjugated—further shrinking, undermining, disrespecting, and fragmenting their sense of self, mind, and body. Reclaiming one's voice, body, and overall agency is a direct response to processing and integrating the feelings and experiences connected to the trauma. By retelling and processing the trauma in a safe space, we begin to take back our voice. By moving, paying attention to, and unlocking parts of our bodies, we begin to release the hold trauma once had on us.

When we reclaim agency and wholeness, the power dynamic shifts. Now the narrative, feelings, and experiences are our own; they no longer belong to those who harmed us or to the traumatic event. Reclaiming agency and wholeness means taking back ourselves, our story, and our childhood by setting boundaries, cultivating resilience, connecting to new and old interests, and developing a new identity that isn't characterized by trauma. The exercises in this chapter are focused on helping you get to this place.

Focusing on Resilience

What You'll Need

- 15 to 60+ minutes of uninterrupted time
- Journal and pen/pencil (or digital)
- Photo of your younger self, a childhood toy (or a reminder of it), or something that represents an interest you had as a child (optional)

Most of us have had moments in our childhood when we spoke up, tried to set boundaries, and felt empowered, confident, and free. However, for those with trauma, these resilient moments and parts of us tend to be overshadowed by the negative experiences. When we reflect and process our childhood, it's difficult to identify positive qualities and experiences. There are survival and evolutionary reasons for this: When there's such a visible pain like trauma, the mind brings all our attention to it so that it can be healed. That's why all our attention tends to go to body discomfort, negative thoughts, or other uncomfortable symptoms. Our body and mind know something is off and that our equilibrium needs to be reset.

Therefore, when we begin to identify and process our trauma, it becomes the most important thing on our minds. The psyche and body focus intensely on the incident. It can even feel as if the incident is happening again, setting off a stress response. However, all of this is an opportunity for us to "undo" that event and gain overall healing. And, as important as it is to validate and grieve these moments, it is just as important to zoom out and get the fuller picture. This means you must create space for *all* your parts, including your resiliency. The goal is to be flexible enough to dance between these parts.

You can begin doing this by reframing your responses to the trauma—understanding that fight, flight, or freeze are survival responses and that these have benefits and a resilient purpose in the moment.

When you identify moments when you also felt resilient, free, and safe, you can start anchoring those moments in your mind so that they become as relevant as the moments when you felt wounded. Furthermore, when you can anchor these resilient moments, you can actualize them and use them as tools in your life now. This helps you develop a complex, flexible view of yourself—you are an individual with extensive experiences that all deserve a seat at the table.

Note The idea here isn't to avoid the trauma but to create space for your resilient parts. This restores your sense of self, incorporates your fragmented parts, and gives you an experiential resource to anchor and ground in. If childhood memories are too triggering right now, you can reflect on a recent time when you were resilient.

Instructions

1. Sit in your calm, quiet space with your journal handy. If you'd like, hang your photo or place your toy or reminder someplace you can see it.

2. Bring to mind three memories from your childhood when you either spoke up for yourself or advocated for yourself by setting boundaries or created space for yourself.

3. In your journal, describe these three moments in detail.

4. Now, zoom in on just the resilient parts. Circle the precise moments when you were resilient and lightly shade out anything that happened prior to the event or afterward.

5. Take three deep breaths and imagine those resilient moments. Think about how you felt empowered, strong, and confident and how you were protecting yourself.

6. As you imagine this event and the feelings connected to it, notice how your body feels when you think of yourself as resilient. Notice your body posture, sensations, and energy at this moment. Sit with these resilient parts, and slowly breathe while affirming each part.

7. To close, take a deep breath and orient yourself to your environment by engaging your five senses.

Journal Prompt

Identify other moments in your childhood or adult life when you displayed resilience. Explore how these resilient parts show up for you now. Reflect on the body sensations connected to this quality.

Writing Your Healing Story

What You'll Need
- 20 to 60+ minutes of uninterrupted time
- Positive memories from childhood
- Journal and pen/pencil (or digital)

The more we explore the resilient parts of us in moments of distress during our childhood, the more visible and accessible they become. As we expand our ability to identify and anchor ourselves in these parts, it becomes easier to connect with and actualize them. They serve as examples and reminders to our psyche that something in us has done this before. Something in us has set boundaries in the past, something in us has spoken up, and something in us has searched for safety. We recognize that there is a voice and sense of self that has been dormant, repressed, or mismanaged, and we try to bring this part back to life.

In addition to symptom reduction, one of the most healing experiences our clients share with us is their ability to desire and advocate for their own needs, wants, and overall self. They no longer live a life that focuses on catering to other people's needs. Now, their experiences are as important and valid as others'. This transformation comes from spending significant time identifying and validating their own needs and discovering their own healing voice.

In this exercise, to serve as the basis for your healing story, you will again identify a moment of resilience in your childhood. You'll also identify people and places that, indirectly or directly, made you feel safe and encouraged you to be yourself and to express yourself. Recalling these memories and anchoring yourself in these moments, people, and places of resilience provides a sense of self-confidence and self-reliance and the permission to speak up, which can help you direct and manage yourself in moments of distress.

Note As you now understand, trauma can fragment our perspectives, leaving us with a divided sense of self that usually becomes overwhelmed by and fixated on the harshness of trauma. The goal is to continue to develop your voice and a compassionate, complex view of yourself, to begin seeing your story and yourself from multiple aspects and layers. This gives you the option to be flexible rather than being just stuck in the trauma.

Instructions

1. Sit in your calm, quiet space with your journal handy. Bring to mind all the people (e.g., friend, family member, teacher) and places (e.g., bedroom, place in nature, friend's home, backyard) that made you feel safe, welcomed, and most like yourself during your childhood. Write down as many examples as you can.

2. As you take note of these people and places that supported you, reflect on the image of the space and the appearance of the people.

3. Now, bring to mind the resilient moments you identified in the previous exercise and any other moments when you felt resilient, empowered, confident, strong, and most like yourself. Describe these resilient parts in detail, highlighting their individual characteristics, skills, and energy.

4. Choose one of the safe, welcoming spaces and one of the people you identified in step 2. Imagine being with that person in that safe space during your childhood. Notice the feelings, body sensations, and thoughts that come up for you as hold this image in mind.

5. Think about that time in your life, and write down the problem/trauma you were facing without going into details—just acknowledge the problem by writing it down like a newspaper headline (e.g., Abusive Parents, Death of a Loved One, Parents Are Divorcing, Bullying at School). Take three deep breaths.

6. Now, start writing your healing story:

- Begin with a scene in which your resilient part is most pronounced. Describe this part of you in detail along with the setting: Where are you? Who is around you?

- Describe how this part of you continues to show up to advocate and protect you long after the trauma/problem occurred. Highlight the actions this part of you took after the difficult situation and how it is showing up for you right now.

- Emphasize how you have been making the effort to heal and take care of yourself (e.g., going to therapy, seeking out spirituality/religion, fostering positive relationships, making educational advances, exercising). Reflect on how your resilient parts show up in these moments.

- Describe how you have grown and matured throughout the years, including things you have learned, insights you've gained, and new skills you have that you didn't have during the traumatic event.

- Express your gratitude for these resilient parts as well as for the people and places you identified.

- Conclude your story with a summary of what you have written and close out by offering yourself encouragement as you continue your healing journey. Know that you can add more details to further validate your resilient part anytime.

7. To close, take three deep breaths and orient yourself to your environment by engaging your five senses.

Journal Prompt

How did you feel while doing this exercise? What is your favorite part of the healing story you just wrote? Why is that part your favorite?

Saying Yes to Boundaries

What You'll Need

- 20 to 60+ minutes of uninterrupted time
- Journal and pen/pencil (or digital)

Saying yes to yourself is saying yes to boundaries. However, culturally, we tend to see boundaries as an action of saying no to others or activities. This places too much emphasis on the other person rather than putting the focus on ourselves. Simply saying no skips a step. There's a need in us that deserves to be met and that we must first say yes to before saying no to another. Otherwise, the "no" turns into a defensive action/survival response that is more about the other person than it is about ourselves. In the course of time, boundaries that are solely built on saying no to others without first saying yes to yourself don't last.

As therapists, we've found that people who struggle with boundaries are often really struggling with people-pleasing—the root of which is difficulty validating their own needs, emotions, and experience. The experience of neglecting one's own needs is usually rooted in childhood experiences, especially those in which a caregiver overlooked the child's needs and said yes to other things. The child thereby learned that their needs were not important and that, to survive in that family dynamic, they should deny their needs and satisfy the needs of the caretaker. Consequently, in adulthood, they continue to neglect their own feelings and needs in favor of meeting the needs of others.

In this exercise, you'll learn to set boundaries by first saying yes to your own needs and wants. You will be listening to and validating your feelings and needs, acknowledging the legitimacy of whatever they may be, and recognizing that they are important enough to create space for. In this way, you become the most important person in the equation, and you will learn to pivot from just saying no to others to first saying yes to yourself. Of course you must first recognize your own needs and affirm and validate them. When you make it a point to validate your feelings, needs, and desires and set time aside for them, this part of you gains importance. You reclaim a sense of agency and power and validate your voice and experience.

Note In cases of abuse where survival is paramount, it is perfectly fitting to just say no without taking the time and steps to first validate your feelings. In these moments, you are validating and protecting yourself—appropriately so—and looking out for your own interests. These boundaries are for your immediate safety and well-being.

Instructions

1. Sit in your calm, quiet space with your journal handy. Bring to mind two to three scenarios in which you struggled to set boundaries and write them down.

2. As you reflect on these scenarios, identify one that is connected to a pattern of not setting boundaries at all. If you can't identify such a scenario, choose the scenario that seems most significant to you right now.

3. Take a deep breath, and imagine this memory fully, making it as vivid as possible by identifying any sensory stimuli associated with the memory. What were you seeing, touching, hearing, smelling, and tasting?

4. Take a few deep breaths and settle your body. Reflect on your needs, wants, desires, and feelings at that time. What part of you did you need to say yes to? Write down each need, feeling, desire, etc. Validate and affirm whatever you identified right now by acknowledging and accepting it as valid.

5. As you hold your feelings and needs in mind, take a moment to sit and contemplate them. Notice the body sensations that come up. Validate and affirm those feelings.

6. Reflect and conceptualize a future moment where you may need to set boundaries, ideally a scenario that's somehow connected to the original situation. Imagine taking a step back and identifying what your needs may be in that scenario. Validate and affirm those needs.

7. Now draw two circles side by side, with the left one being double the size of the one on the right (as illustrated below). In the left circle, write down all your needs and wants. In the right circle, write down who or what you are having trouble saying no to.

8. Take a moment to reflect and contemplate the circles. Visualize yourself setting the boundaries and saying no in the future scenario.

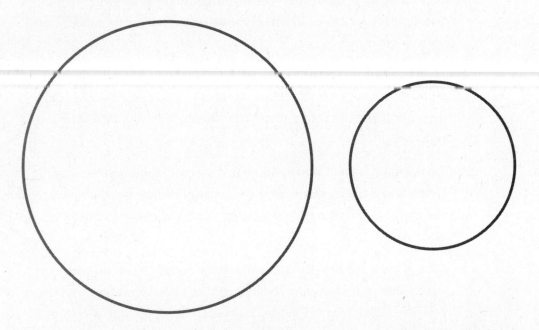

9. To close, take three deep breaths and orient yourself to your environment by engaging your five senses.

Journal Prompt

Reflect and analyze why you may struggle with setting boundaries. When did this people-pleasing behavior begin for you and why did this part of you emerge? Reflect on what parts and needs of yours went neglected in those early moments and triggered the people-pleasing behaviors.

Reconnecting to Playfulness

What You'll Need

- 30 to 60+ minutes of uninterrupted time
- Journal and pen/pencil (or digital)

Play is often one of our earliest experiences of connection and safety. However, when we become adults, many of us trade in play for a life of busyness that's often rife with stress and anxiety. This is partly out of our control; demands and expectations of adulthood can suck the fun and play out of us. Consequently, over time, our inner child becomes foggier, hidden, or only associated with generalized monotone views of self, either as a wounded child or a perfect one. As we know, we are much more complex than that; our lives have been full of experiences, some of them unpredictable, others mundane, others pleasurable, others fun, good, bad, etc. All these experiences are better faced and managed when we are emotionally and intellectually more flexible and able to create a balance between self-care and interacting with our environment.

So how do we facilitate emotional and intellectual flexibility, self-care, reduced stress, social improvement, and connectedness with others while connecting with our inner child? As you will discover in this exercise, the answer is to engage with play and/or reconnect with a childhood interest.

Most of us engaged in childhood play in some way, even those among us with an extended history of trauma. Again, it's essential to acknowledge the fullness of our whole self. We want to create space and give voice to the wounded parts of us as well as to all the other parts of us, including the resilient part and the playful part. Reengaging with childhood interests and play helps cultivate a sense of freedom, confidence, joy, imagination, creativity, and problem-solving while relieving stress and anxiety.

Clinically, engaging with play or childhood interests reenacts a pattern experienced during childhood similar to those horrible experiences of reliving our trauma, but this time, we are reliving moments of safety, connection, creativity, newness, and freedom, highlighting and sending a reminder to our psyche that this part of us is also important enough to have a seat at the table. Additionally, if play is done with others, we can heal attachment wounds, improve socially, bond, and grow relationally.

Note Many professions, like sports, acting, and the arts, are connected to a sense of play, creativity, and fun. When asked what they want to be when they grow up, many children will identify one of these professions, fantasizing that play will continue into their adulthood. Now is your chance to affirm that part of yourself by engaging in play. More important than the type of activity you choose for this exercise is establishing a consistent pattern of play.

Instructions

1. Sit in your calm, quiet space with your journal handy. Bring to mind a moment during your childhood when you engaged in play. Some examples include playing board games with friends, playing with toys, building with connecting blocks, riding bikes, playing sports, climbing on playground equipment, and so on.

2. No matter how big or small the activity was, remember how you felt free, safe, and unbothered during that time of play. Describe the type of play in your journal.

3. Now sit with this moment. Visualize your younger self playing. Imagine this memory fully, making it as vivid as possible by identifying any sensory stimuli associated with the memory. What were you seeing, touching, hearing, smelling, and tasting?

4. Notice the body sensations, feelings, and energies that come up for you as you hold this image of your inner child playing. Validate and affirm these sensations and feelings you now hold in your body.

5. Take a deep breath, and orient yourself to your present environment by engaging your five senses.

6. Now brainstorm two to three activities/interests that can help you engage with your sense of play. Some examples include making a favorite treat you enjoyed making (or helped make) as a child, playing an instrument you used to play, playing a retro board game, reconnecting with a childhood friend, dancing and singing, doing something artistic, or playing a sport.

7. Take out your calendar and schedule in one or more of those activities each week. Set an intention to pencil in play on a weekly basis.

Journal Prompt

What feelings and body sensations came up for you during the exercise? What feelings may surface when you reconnect to play now?

Imagining Your Future Whole Self

What You'll Need

- 20 to 60+ minutes of uninterrupted time
- Journal and pen/pencil (or digital)

The ability to visualize a healed, wise, and restored part of yourself is affirming and stabilizing. Many therapeutic approaches and schools of thought, including EMDR, mindfulness, Internal Family Systems, Jungian analysis, and positive psychology, have supported folks in seeing a part of themselves that's whole, sound, and full of agency. This part of self is typically an imagined future self who is older and holds healing information for our current self (an inner advisor, if you will). However, there's a gap between our current state and who we hope to be when we reach a certain age or milestone.

At times, it's hard to access this inner advisor without materializing it through language, art, or positive projections. In this exercise, you'll conjure up a mental image of your future whole self to make communication with this part easier. Imagining your future whole self opens the door, not just to dream but to anticipate this part of you eventually existing. When you see, think, and feel something repeatedly, even if it's just in your mind, you begin to normalize it and expect it to occur. This process builds confidence and lays out an easier path for you to achieve your goals while also beginning to cultivate the inner voice of your future whole self. This voice and sense of self, which seems far away, will begin to feel more familiar and accessible, and eventually, it will be a part of who you are now.

Childhood trauma can fragment our sense of self and time, as well as our ability to imagine. This is why a huge part of trauma therapy is bringing those parts up again—be they the wounded inner child, the resilient younger self, or the future whole self—and highlighting, validating, reestablishing, and ultimately defragmenting them. This means that once all your parts are seen, noticed, loved, and integrated into your being, they are whole and supported by you.

The ability to be present while acknowledging your past and future selves gives you a wide overview of who you are. Think of it this way: You'll always have one foot in the present moment, while the other foot steps back into the past to reflect and process and then steps forward into the future to dream, hope, and set goals. The ability to hold the complexity of self will support you in holding and managing the complexities of your emotions, physical and mental states, and even your trauma-related symptoms. Hopefully, this ability draws you to a place where you begin to see yourself through a compassionate lens.

Note You do not need to make the image you conjure up complicated or detailed. Start with the first image that comes to mind. It does not have to resemble you at all; this is more about targeting a feeling than a particular appearance. If the feeling and ideas of your future self are experienced in your body and thoughts, an image will likely appear.

Instructions

1. Sit in your calm, quiet space. Take a deep breath, close your eyes or gaze down, and think about a place you associate with peace and calmness. This can be the safe place you identified in the exercise on page 51 or it can be a different place, real or fictitious. This is where you will encounter your future whole self.

2. Bring the safe place fully to life and ground yourself in it by acknowledging your five senses: Name five things you can see, four things you can touch, three things you can hear, two things you can smell,

and one thing you can taste in this place. Hold this image in mind for at least 30 seconds.

3. Now, imagine your future whole self slowly showing up in your safe place. Let them appear at their own pace; do not rush the process. As they show up, notice how they look in whatever detail you can. What stands out about their appearance—clothing, body, hair, face, etc.?

4. Move closer to your future whole self and introduce yourself. Tell them about the healing work you've been doing and what else is going on.

5. Ask your future whole self any question you would like an answer to, and then listen for an answer. Make a mental note of whatever comes to you.

6. Give yourself at least two minutes to be with your future whole self, even if it's in silence. When you feel your time with them is complete, thank them for showing up.

7. To close, ground yourself to your present environment by engaging your five senses.

Journal Prompt

Describe what your future whole self looks like. What are they like emotionally and physically? What feelings came up for you while you were with them? Reflect on the question you asked your future whole self and explore the meaning of their answer.

CONCLUSION

Congratulations on working through this book. It takes tremendous courage to confront some of the pain, emotions, and memories associated with childhood trauma. We extend to you our heartfelt appreciation and gratitude for your dedication to your healing.

Remember that the healing process is not linear. It is important to notice and celebrate small moments of progress along the way. We suggest you continue to revisit the exercises in this book as needed and feel free to modify the exercises to better fit your needs. There's an old Afro-Brazilian saying that goes, "If you go back to the water, you will continue to be nourished." Our hope is that you will continue to nourish yourself with the comfort and connection you deserve.

The part of you that believed in your capacity to heal your traumatic wounds is the healing power within you. Carry on by cultivating this desire to heal from childhood trauma by giving this part of you—and *all* of you—permission to continue to widen, expand, and evolve. As you grow and navigate the unpredictability of life, identify anchors along the way and seek a deep, loving connection between yourself and others.

RESOURCES

Podcasts

House of Therapy Podcast with Sostenes and Erica Lima
www.open.spotify.com/show/5iQEV1PU9fThsTDzAPOUG1
podcasts.apple.com/us/podcast/house-of-therapy/id1727963910

IFS Talks Podcast with Aníbal Henriques, Tisha Shull, and Alexia Rothman
www.podcasts.apple.com/us/podcast/ifs-talks/id1481000501
open.spotify.com/show/5vDQSPfZm6mgWTLJZU0X0q

Latinx Therapy with Adriana Alejandre, LMFT
www.latinxtherapy.com/podcast

Stuck Not Broken with Justin Sunseri, LMFT
www.justinlmft.com/podcast

Therapy Chat with Laura Reagan, LCSW-C
www.podcasts.apple.com/us/podcast/therapy-chat/id1031099411

The Trauma Therapist Project with Guy MacPherson, PhD
www.thetraumatherapistproject.com/podcast

Books

Accessing the Healing Power of the Vagus Nerve: Self-Help Exercises for Anxiety, Depression, Trauma, and Autism by Stanley Rosenberg (Berkeley, CA: North Atlantic Books, 2017)

The Body Keeps the Score: Brain, Mind, and Body in the Healing of Trauma by Bessel van der Kolk, MD (New York: Penguin Books, 2014)

The Boy Who Was Raised as a Dog: And Other Stories from a Child Psychiatrist's Notebook: What Traumatized Children Can Teach Us about

Love, Loss, and Healing by Bruce D. Perry, MD, PhD, and Maia Szalavitz (New York: Hachette Book Group, 2017)

Collected Works of C. G. Jung, Volume 9 (Part 1): The Archetypes and the Collective Unconscious by C. G. Jung, translated by R. F. C. Hull (Princeton, NJ: Princeton University Press, 1980)

Complex PTSD: From Surviving to Thriving: A Guide and Map for Recovering from Childhood Trauma by Pete Walker (Azure Coyote, 2013)

Cultural Competence and Healing Culturally Based Trauma with EMDR Therapy: Innovative Strategies and Protocols, edited by Mark Nickerson (New York: Springer Publishing Company, 2017)

The Deepest Well: Healing the Long-Term Effects of Childhood Adversity by Nadine Burke Harris, MD (New York: Houghton Mifflin Harcourt, 2018)

Divergent Mind: Thriving in a World That Wasn't Designed For You by Jenara Nerenberg (New York: HarperCollins Publishers, 2021)

Emotional Inheritance: A Therapist, Her Patients, and the Legacy of Trauma by Galit Atlas, PhD (New York: Little, Brown Spark, 2022)

Eye Movement Desensitization and Reprocessing (EMDR) Therapy: Basic Principles, Protocols, and Procedures, Third Edition, by Francine Shapiro, PhD (New York: The Guilford Press, 2018)

Healing Trauma: A Pioneering Program for Restoring the Wisdom of Your Body by Peter A. Levine, PhD (Boulder, CO: Sounds True, 2008)

Healing Trauma: Attachment, Mind, Body, and Brain, edited by Marion F. Solomon, PhD, and Daniel J. Siegel, MD (New York: W. W. Norton & Company, 2003)

In an Unspoken Voice: How the Body Releases Trauma and Restores Goodness by Peter A. Levine, PhD (Berkeley, CA: North Atlantic Books, 2010)

The Internal Family Systems (IFS) Flip Chart: A Psychoeducational Tool for Unlocking the Incredible Healing Potential of the Multiple Mind by Colleen West, LMFT (Eau Claire, WI: PESI Publishing, 2023)

Internal Family Systems Therapy: Supervision and Consultation by Emma E. Redfern (New York: Routledge, 2023)

It Didn't Start with You: How Inherited Family Trauma Shapes Who We Are and How to End the Cycle by Mark Wolynn (New York: Penguin Books, 2016)

My Grandmother's Hands: Racialized Trauma and the Pathway to Mending Our Hearts and Bodies by Resmaa Menakem, MSW, LICSW, SEP (Las Vegas, NV: Central Recovery Press, 2017)

No Bad Parts: Healing Trauma and Restoring Wholeness with the Internal Family Systems Model by Richard C. Schwartz, PhD (Boulder, CO: Sounds True, 2021)

The Pain We Carry: Healing from Complex PTSD for People of Color by Natalie Y. Gutiérrez, LMFT (Oakland, CA: New Harbinger Publications, 2022)

Playing and Reality, 2nd edition, by D. W. Winnicott (New York: Routledge Classics, 2005)

Polyvagal Exercises for Safety and Connection: 50 Client-Centered Practices by Deb Dana (New York: W. W. Norton & Company, 2020)

The Polyvagal Theory in Therapy: Engaging the Rhythm of Regulation by Deb Dana (New York: W. W. Norton & Company, 2018)

The Practical Guide for Healing Developmental Trauma: Using the Neuro-Affective Relational Model to Address Adverse Childhood Experiences and Resolve Complex Trauma by Laurence Heller, PhD, and Brad J. Kammer, LMFT (Berkeley, CA: North Atlantic Books, 2022)

Somatic Internal Family Systems Therapy: Awareness, Breath, Resonance, Movement, and Touch in Practice by Susan McConnell (Berkeley, CA: North Atlantic Books, 2020)

Too Loud, Too Bright, Too Fast, Too Tight: What to Do If You Are Sensory Defensive in an Overstimulating World by Sharon Heller, PhD (New York: Harper Perennial, 2003)

Trauma and Attachment: Over 150 Attachment-Based Interventions to Heal Trauma by Christina Reese, PhD, LCPC (Eau Claire, WI: PESI Publishing, 2021)

Trauma and Recovery: The Aftermath of Violence—from Domestic Abuse to Political Terror by Judith L. Herman, MD (New York: Basic Books, 2022)

Trauma and the Body: A Sensorimotor Approach to Psychotherapy by Pat Ogden, Kekuni Minton, and Clare Pain (New York: W. W. Norton and Company, 2006)

Trauma Through a Child's Eyes: Awakening the Ordinary Miracle of Healing by Peter A. Levine, PhD, and Maggie Kline, MS, MFT (Berkeley, CA: North Atlantic Books, 2019, and Lyons, CO: ERGOS Institute Press, 2019)

Truth and Repair: How Trauma Survivors Envision Justice by Judith L. Herman, MD (New York: Basic Books, 2023)

Waking the Tiger: Healing Trauma by Peter A. Levine, PhD, with Ann Frederick (Berkeley, CA: North Atlantic Books, 1997)

What Happened to You?: Conversations on Trauma, Resilience, and Healing by Bruce D. Perry, MD, PhD, and Oprah Winfrey (New York: Flatiron Books, 2021)

What My Bones Know: A Memoir of Healing from Complex Trauma by Stephanie Foo (New York: Ballantine Books, 2022)

When the Body Says No: Exploring the Stress-Disease Connection by Gabor Maté, MD (Hoboken, NJ: John Wiley & Sons, 2011)

The Wisdom of Your Body: Finding Healing, Wholeness, and Connection Through Embodied Living by Hillary L. McBride, PhD (Grand Rapids, MI: Brazos Press, 2021)

Websites

American Academy of Experts in Traumatic Stress (aaets.org)

Asian-American Health Initiative: Resource Library (aahiinfo.org/aahi-resources)

Black Emotional and Mental Health Collective: Wellness Tools (beam.community/wellness-tools)

Center for the Study of Traumatic Stress (cstsonline.org)

David Baldwin's Trauma Information Pages (trauma-pages.com)

Frances Booth, LICSW (francesbooth.com)

The Highly Sensitive Person (hsperson.com)

Julie Bjelland: Empowering the Highly Sensitive & Neurodiverse People (juliebjelland.com)

Latinx Therapy: Latinx Therapists & Speakers (latinxtherapy.com)

National Queer & Trans Therapists of Color Network (nqttcn.com/en)

Somatic IFS: Susan McConnell, MA, CHT (embodiedself.net)

Substance Abuse and Mental Health Services Administration: Programs (samhsa.gov/programs)

White Bison: Culturally Based Healing to Indigenous People (whitebison.org)

REFERENCES

Chapter 2

Cook, Alexandra, Joseph Spinazzola, Julian Ford, Cheryl Lanktree, Margaret Blaustein, Marylene Cloitre, Ruth DeRosa, et al. "Complex Trauma in Children and Adolescents." *Psychiatric Annals* 35, no. 5 (May 2005): 390–398. doi:10.3928/00485713-20050501-05.

PESI Inc. "5 Essential Moves of the EFT Tango with Dr. Sue Johnson." Posted September 21, 2016. YouTube video, 8:09. www.youtube.com/watch?v=gZ7ELF8mE3Q.

Spinazzola, Joseph. "PTSD: The Tip of the Iceberg in Adaptation to Complex Trauma." Accessed November 30, 2023. www.complextrauma.org/complex-trauma/ptsd-tip-of-iceberg-in-adaptation-to-complex-trauma.

Chapter 3

Mindful Staff. "The Science of Mindfulness." Mindful.org. August 31, 2022. Accessed September 10, 2023. www.mindful.org/the-science-of-mindfulness.

Nguyen, Jessica, and Eric Brymer. (October 2, 2018). "Nature-Based Guided Imagery as an Intervention for State Anxiety." *Frontiers in Psychology* 9 (October 2018): 1858. doi: 10.3389/fpsyg.2018.01858.

Van der Veer, Peter. "Global Breathing." *Max Planck Institute for the Study of Religious and Ethnic Diversity* blog. April 24, 2020. Accessed September 10, 2023. www.mmg.mpg.de/570525/blog-vanderveer-global-breathing.

Zimmerman, Thomas. "A Script for Developing, Practicing, and Using Attachment Figure Resources in EMDR Therapy." *Go With That* (blog). February 9, 2022. Accessed September 11, 2023. gowiththat.wordpress.com/2022/02/09/attachment.

Chapter 5

Bickham, Samantha, LMHC. "What Is Fight, Flight, Freeze, Fawn?" Choosing Therapy. June 19, 2023. Accessed October 3, 2023. www.choosingtherapy.com/fight-flight-freeze-fawn.

Hippe, Hannah. "Being Lonely and Being Alone: What's the Difference?" Nystrom and Associates. February 4, 2021. Accessed September 22, 2023. www.nystromcounseling.com/grief-loss/being-lonely-and-being-alone-whats-the-difference.

Seppälä, Emma, PhD. "The Brain's Ability to Look Within: A Secret to Self-Mastery." *Psychology Today*. December 10, 2012. Accessed October 9, 2023. www.psychologytoday.com/us/blog/feeling-it/201212/the-brains-ability-look-within-secret-self-mastery.

Van der Kolk, Bessel, MD. *The Body Keeps the Score: Brain, Mind, and Body in the Healing of Trauma*. (New York: Penguin Books, 2014)

Chapter 7

Barlow, M. Rose, Cory Anne Hutchinson, Kelsey Newton, Tess Grover, and Lindsey Ward. "Childhood Neglect, Attachment to Companion Animals, and Stuffed Animals as Attachment Objects in Women and Men." *Anthrozoös* 25, no. 1 (March 2012): 111–119. doi:10.2752/175303712X13240472427159.

Van der Kolk, Bessel, MD. *The Body Keeps the Score: Brain, Mind, and Body in the Healing of Trauma*. (New York: Penguin Books, 2014)

INDEX

ACKNOWLEDGMENTS

We would like to take a moment of gratitude to acknowledge the people, places, and organizations that helped us bring this book to life.

On behalf of our organization's birthplace and its current home, we must first acknowledge the unceded territory of the Tongva (Gabrieleño) and Acjachemen (Juaneño) people, who have lived and stewarded the land before us and continue to live in Long Beach, California, and the unceded territory of the Cheraw, Mánu: Yį Įsuwą, Waxhaw, and Sugaree people, who have lived and stewarded the land before us and continue to live in Charlotte, North Carolina. We honor and acknowledge all that you have preserved and given to the community that has not been fully seen or acknowledged.

We would like to express our deepest love and gratitude to each other, for the motivation, support, and care throughout this process of writing. In the same vein, we would like to thank our family, especially our three kiddos, Iris, Raynah, and Ruben, who were flexible, excited, and inspiring.

A special thanks to our editor, Clara Song Lee, and the folks at Zeitgeist and Penguin Random House, who believed in us and supportively walked alongside us in this process.

We extend our appreciation to those who have done this work before us, the people who spent hours training and supervising us, our colleagues, and most of all our clients—all these individuals in their own unique ways have pushed us to be more compassionate, curious, and resilient in this work.

Finally, we want to express our gratitude to you, the reader, who has taken the time to reflect, digest, and do your own healing work. You are an inspiration to us all. Thank you!

ABOUT THE AUTHORS

 **Sostenes B. Lima, LCSW,** is a licensed therapist who specializes in working with trauma survivors. He holds a master's degree in advanced clinical social work from Columbia University and a bachelor of science in psychology from Grand Canyon University. Sostenes has extensive training in psychodynamic and attachment-based therapy and incorporates trauma-focused therapeutic modalities such as EMDR, mindfulness, and somatic-based therapies into his practice. His integrative approach to therapy is tailored to meet each person's needs in a warm, inviting, safe space where they can connect, process, and heal.

Born in Rio de Janeiro, Sostenes immigrated to Miami, Florida, at the age of eight. As a mixed-race individual of Afro-Brazilian, Indigenous Brazilian, and Portuguese descent, he embodies a rich tapestry of cultural influences and maintains a profound appreciation for the diversity of human experiences. Sostenes is also an artist, father, and partner who deeply respects the intricate paths people navigate in their healing journeys.

To learn more, visit sunsettraumatherapy.com and follow him on Instagram @sostenes.lima.lcsw.

Erica Lima, LCSW, is a licensed therapist who specializes in working with people who have experienced trauma and childhood neglect and who struggle with people-pleasing, perfectionism, relationship OCD, and more. She holds a bachelor's degree in social work from the University of North Carolina at Charlotte and a master's degree in social work from Arizona State University. Erica has received specialized training in Emotion-Focused Couples Therapy (EFCT), Internal Family Systems Therapy (IFS), Somatic Parts Work (IFS) with Level 3 Certification, Somatic Attachment Therapy, Hakomi therapy, and Cultural Somatics for Racial Equity. Her integrative approach is founded on a strength-based, trauma-informed, and anti-oppressive perspective, acknowledging the impact of systemic oppression on marginalized communities, and prioritizing a safe, anti-discriminatory environment in therapy. She takes great care and values mutual trust in working with people of color. She also supports white individuals seeking to heal from internalized white supremacy.

Raised on the outskirts of Charlotte, North Carolina, Erica now cherishes the beauty of the vibrant city life. Her passion is to support those in the helping professions and others on a path to loving themselves more fully and cultivating genuine connections in their relationships.

Sostenes and Erica own and operate Sunset Trauma Therapy, a private practice based in California and North Carolina, where they work with individuals and couples to address experiences of trauma, PTSD, anxiety, depression, family-of-origin conflicts, self-esteem issues, burnout and compassion fatigue, grief and loss, parental stress, relationship difficulties, mood disorders, and more.

To learn more, visit sunsettraumatherapy.com and follow her on Instagram @ericalimalcsw.

Hi there,

We hope you found *Overcoming Your Childhood Trauma* helpful. If you have any questions or concerns about your book, or have received a damaged copy, please contact customerservice@penguinrandomhouse.com. We're here and happy to help.

Also, please consider writing a review on your favorite retailer's website to let others know what you thought of the book.

Sincerely,
The Zeitgeist Team